SRA Spelling

Dr. Nancy L. Roser
Professor, Language and Literacy Studies
The University of Texas
College of Education
Austin, Texas

Dr. Jean Wallace Gillet
Reading Specialist
Charlottesville Public Schools
Charlottesville, VA

SRA McGraw-Hill

Columbus, Ohio

A Division of The McGraw·Hill Companies

Program Reviewers

Wendy Fries
Teacher GATE Coordinator
Kings River Union School District
Kingsburg, CA

Cynthia W. Gardner
Exceptional Children's Teacher
Balls Creek Elementary School
Newton, NC

Diane Jones
Teacher
East Clayton Elementary School
Clayton, NC

Sheryl Kurtin
Curriculum Teacher
Tuttle Elementary School
Sarasota, FL

Ann Ogburn
Curriculum Coordinator
Johnston County Schools
Smithfield, NC

Michael Reck
Teacher
Big Walnut Schools
Sunbury, OH

Dr. Sherry V. Reynolds
Classroom Teacher/Elementary
 Curriculum Specialist
Will Rogers Elementary School
Stillwater, OK

Illustrations: Olivia Cole, Steve McInturff, Sherry Neidigh, Sue Parnell

www.sra4kids.com

SRA/McGraw-Hill

A Division of The McGraw·Hill Companies

Send all inquiries to:
SRA/McGraw-Hill
8787 Orion Place
Columbus, Ohio 43240-4027

Printed in the United States of America.

ISBN 0-07-572284-4

3 4 5 6 7 8 9 QPD 07 06 05 04

How to Study a Word

1 **Look** at the word.   **print**
    What does it mean?
    How is it spelled?

2 **Say** the word.   **print**
    What sounds do you hear?
    Are there any silent letters?

3 **Think** about the word.   **pr i nt**
    How is each sound spelled?
    Do you see any word parts?

4 **Write** the word.   **print**
    Did you copy all the letters
        carefully?
    Did you think about the sounds
        and letters?

5 **Check** the spelling.   **print**
    Did you spell the word
        correctly?
    Do you need to write it again?

Contents

UNIT 4

UNIT 5

UNIT 6

Student Handbook

1

The Letters
I, L, T, K, Y, Z, V, W, X

i l L l

x z y z

W z x W

VISUALIZATION STRATEGY
Circle the letters
that are the same.

T t k t

k X K K

v V w v

T I t I

Y Z Z z

y k y Y

PRONUNCIATION STRATEGY
Name the letter.
Trace the letter.
Write the letter.

I   I

i   i

L   L

l   l

T   T

t   t

PRONUNCIATION STRATEGY
Name the letter.
Trace the letter.
Write the letter.

K K

k k

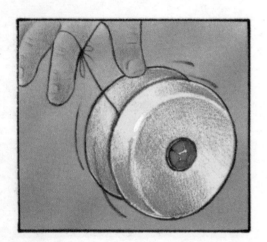

Y Y

y y

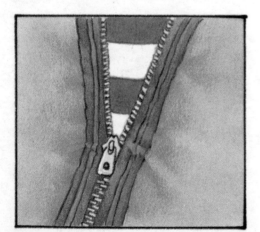

Z Z

z z

PRONUNCIATION STRATEGY
Name the letter.
Trace the letter.
Write the letter.

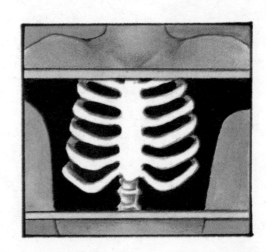

2

The Letters O, C, U, S, J, G, P, B, D

VISUALIZATION STRATEGY
Circle the letters that are the same.

U O u U

s s c o

P B D P

J G g J

B d b d

j g p p

O u U O

c C O C

d b b p

![icon] **PRONUNCIATION STRATEGY**
Name the letter.
Trace the letter.
Write the letter.

O O

o o

C C

c c

U U

u u

PRONUNCIATION STRATEGY
Name the letter.
Trace the letter.
Write the letter.

S S

s s

J J

j j

G G

g g

Name the letter.
Trace the letter.
Write the letter.

P P _____

p p _____

B B _____

b b _____

D D _____

d d _____

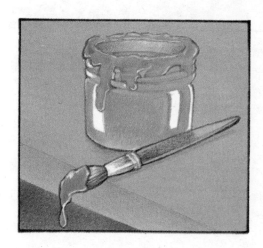

The Letters
H, M, N, A,
E, Q, R, F

HNNM

fFhh

VISUALIZATION STRATEGY
**Circle the letters
that are the same.**

rrRF

QQEF

mMnm

aeAa

frRf

EFeE

aqeq

PRONUNCIATION STRATEGY
Name the letter.
Trace the letter.
Write the letter.

H H

h h

M M

m m

N N

n n

PRONUNCIATION STRATEGY
Name the letter.
Trace the letter.
Write the letter.

A A

a a

E E

e e

Q Q

q q

PRONUNCIATION STRATEGY
Name the letter.
Trace the letter.
Write the letter.

Ff Rr Oo Mm

Beginning Consonant Sounds /t/, /m/, /s/, /j/, /k/

PRONUNCIATION STRATEGY
Name the pictures.
Match the beginning sounds.

PRONUNCIATION STRATEGY
Name the picture.
Circle the beginning letter.

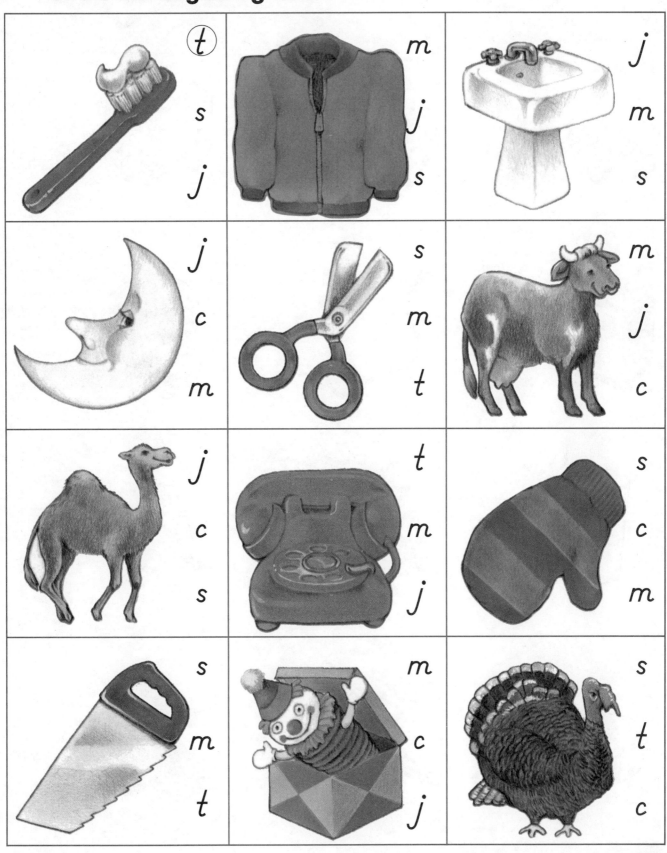

(t) s j	m j s	j m s
j c m	s m t	m j c
j c s	t m j	s c m
s m t	m c j	s t c

PRONUNCIATION STRATEGY
Name the picture.
Write the beginning letter.

t m s j c

c

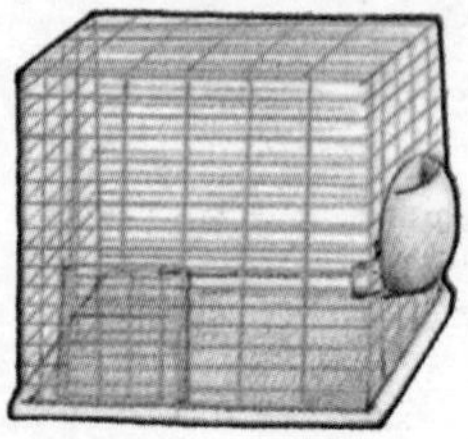

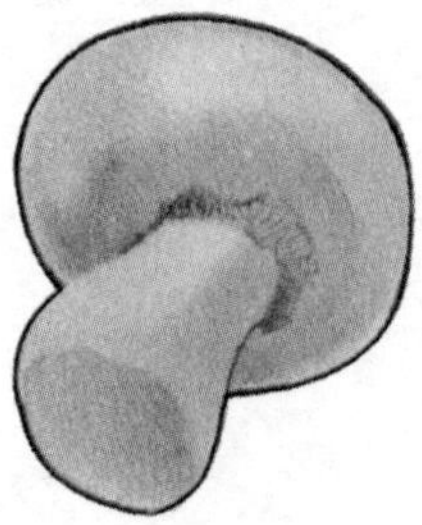

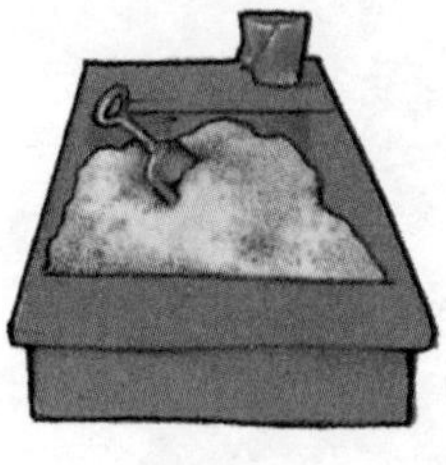

PRONUNCIATION STRATEGY
Name the picture.
Write the beginning letter.

t m s j c

can

ar

op

op

up

un

5

Beginning Consonant Sounds
/d/, /f/, /g/, /n/, /w/

 PRONUNCIATION STRATEGY
Name the pictures.
Match the beginning sounds.

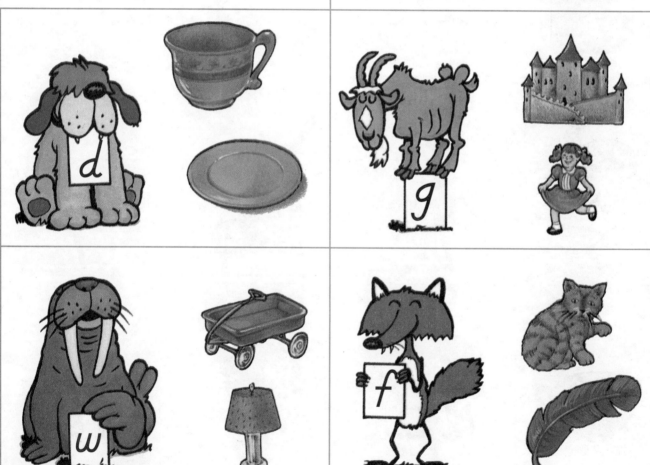

PRONUNCIATION STRATEGY
Name the picture.
Circle the beginning letter.

PRONUNCIATION STRATEGY
Name the picture.
Write the beginning letter.

d f g n w

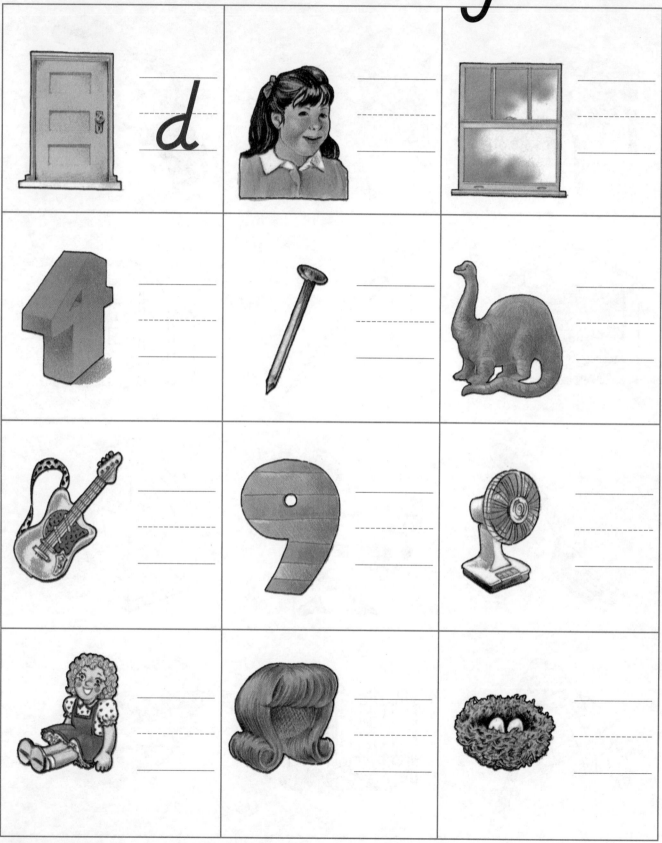

d

Beginning Consonant Sounds /d/, /f/, /g/, /n/, /w/

PRONUNCIATION STRATEGY
Name the picture.
Write the beginning letter.

d f g n w

nut

og

ig

ox

as

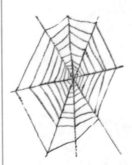

eb

6

Beginning Consonant Sounds /b/, /h/, /p/, /r/

 PRONUNCIATION STRATEGY
Name the pictures.
Match the beginning sounds.

PRONUNCIATION STRATEGY
Name the picture.
Circle the beginning letter.

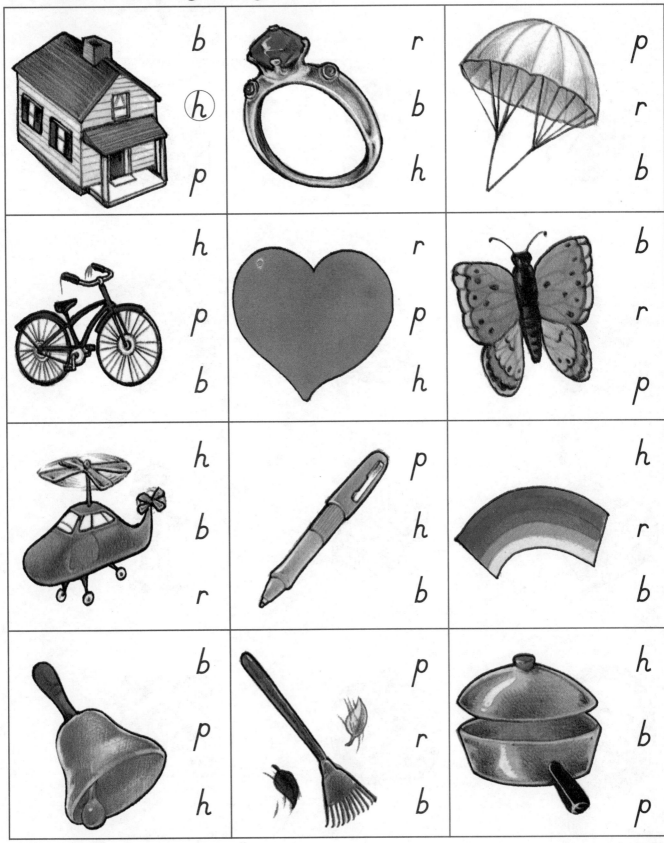

PRONUNCIATION STRATEGY
Name the picture.
Write the beginning letter.

b h p r

b

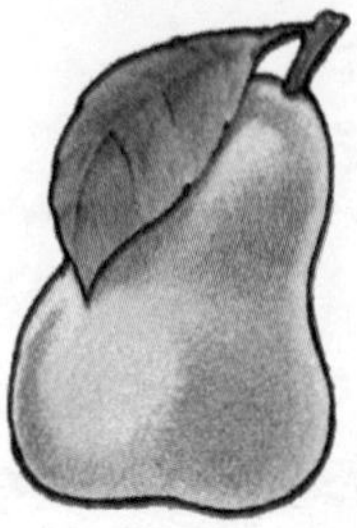

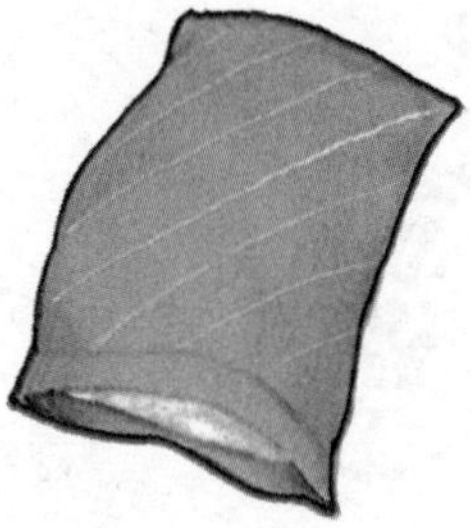

Beginning Consonant Sounds /b/, /h/, /p/, /r/

PRONUNCIATION STRATEGY
Name the picture.
Write the beginning letter.

b h p r

hen

ot

ox

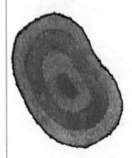

ug

ed

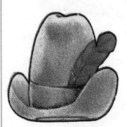

at

7

Beginning Consonant Sounds
/k/, /l/, /v/, /y/, /z/

PRONUNCIATION STRATEGY
Name the pictures.
Match the beginning sounds.

PRONUNCIATION STRATEGY
Name the picture.
Circle the beginning letter.

(k) l v	y z k	l v y
z k l	v y z	k l v
y z k	l v y	z k l
v y z	k l v	y z k

PRONUNCIATION STRATEGY
Name the picture.
Write the beginning letter.

k l v y z

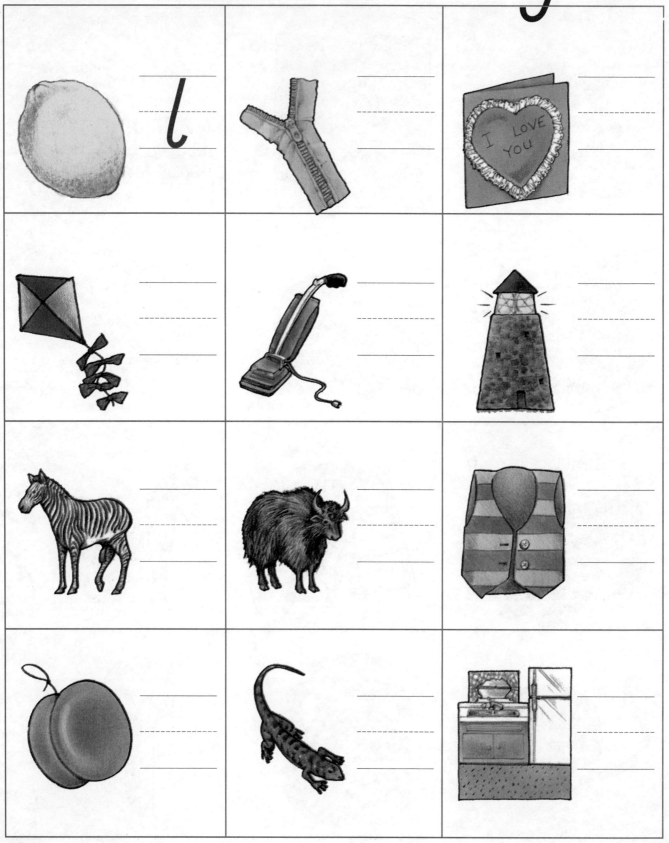

PRONUNCIATION STRATEGY
Name the picture.
Write the beginning letter.

k l v y z

 yak	 iss
 id	 an
 oo	 og

Ending Consonant Sounds /d/, /t/, /m/

 PRONUNCIATION STRATEGY
Name the pictures.
Match the ending sounds.

PRONUNCIATION STRATEGY
Name the picture.
Circle the ending letter.

(t) m d	m d t	d t m
m d t	d t m	t m d
d t m	t m d	m d t
t m d	m d t	d t m

PRONUNCIATION STRATEGY
Name the picture.
Write the ending letter.

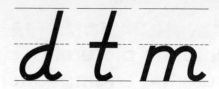

t		

PRONUNCIATION STRATEGY
Name the picture.
Write the ending letter.

d t m

jam

pa

re

ca

mo

je

Ending Consonant Sounds /s/, /g/, /b/

 PRONUNCIATION STRATEGY
Name the pictures.
Match the ending sounds.

PRONUNCIATION STRATEGY
Name the picture.
Circle the ending letter.

(b) g s	s b g	g b s
s g b	b s g	s b g
g s b	s g b	g b s
b s g	b g s	s b g

PRONUNCIATION STRATEGY
Name the picture.
Write the ending letter.

s g b

PRONUNCIATION STRATEGY
Name the picture.
Write the ending letter.

s g b

log

ga

bi

bu

bu

tu

10
Ending Consonant Sounds
/p/, /n/, /x/

 PRONUNCIATION STRATEGY
Name the pictures.
Match the ending sounds.

PRONUNCIATION STRATEGY
Name the picture.
Circle the ending letter.

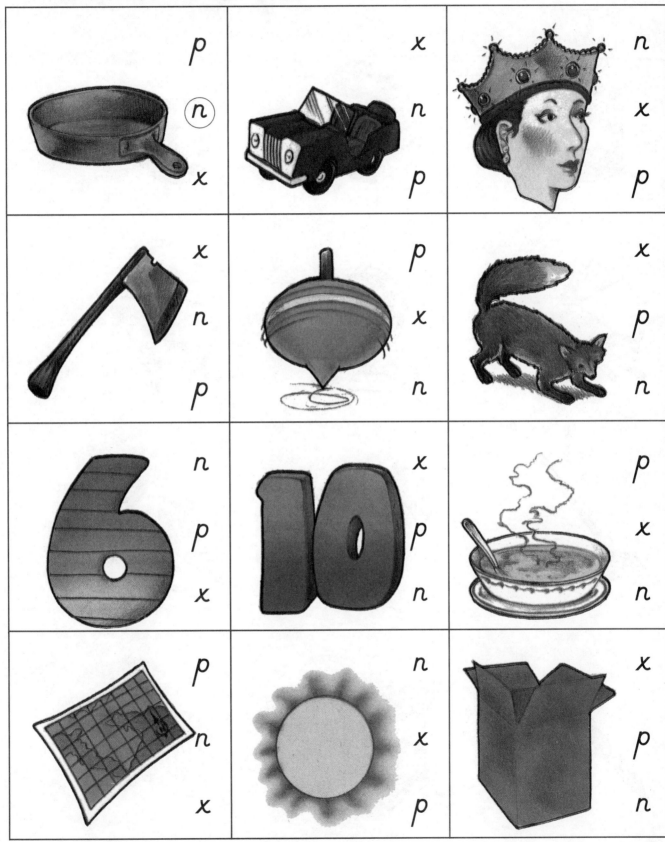

p (n) x	x n p	n x p
x n p	p x n	x p n
n p x	x p n	p x n
p n x	n x p	x p n

PRONUNCIATION STRATEGY
Name the picture.
Write the ending letter.

p n x

 n

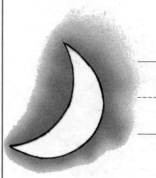

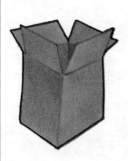

Ending Consonant Sounds /p/, /n/, /x/

 PRONUNCIATION STRATEGY
Name the picture.
Write the ending letter.

p n x

 *van*

 *bo*

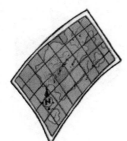 *ma*

 *si*

 *cu*

 *pa*

11

The /a/ Sound

PRONUNCIATION STRATEGY
Say the words.
Circle the pictures
with the same
middle sound as

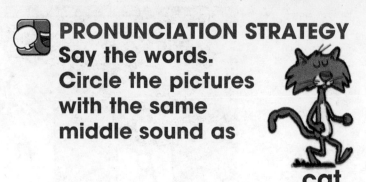

cat

PRONUNCIATION STRATEGY
Name the pictures.
Match the middle sounds.

PRONUNCIATION STRATEGY
Name the picture.
Listen for the /a/ sound.
Write the letter a.

The /a/ Sound

a

PRONUNCIATION STRATEGY
Name the picture.
Write the letter.

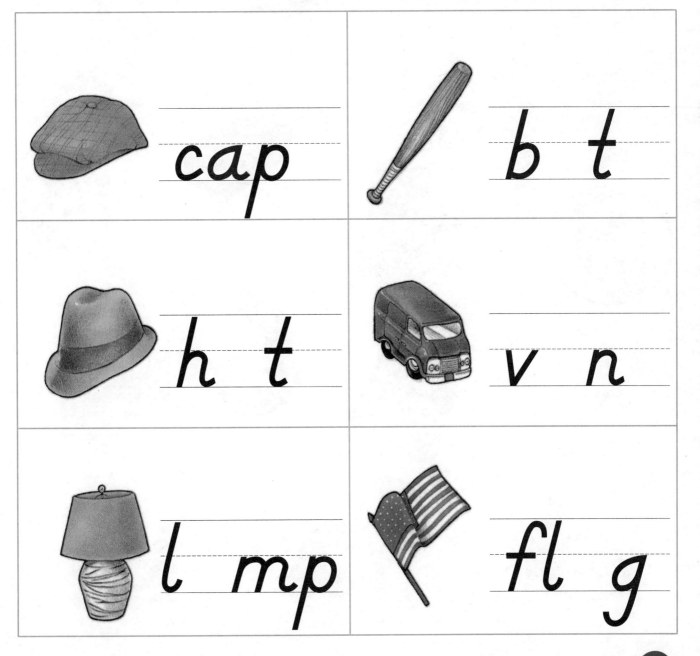

cap

b___t

h___t

v___n

l___mp

fl___g

12

The /i/ Sound

 PRONUNCIATION STRATEGY
Name the pictures.
Circle the ones with
the same middle
sound as

pig

PRONUNCIATION STRATEGY
Name the pictures.
Match the middle sounds.

PRONUNCIATION STRATEGY
Name the picture. Listen for the
/i/ sound. Write the letter *i*.

i

PRONUNCIATION STRATEGY
Name the picture.
Write the letter.

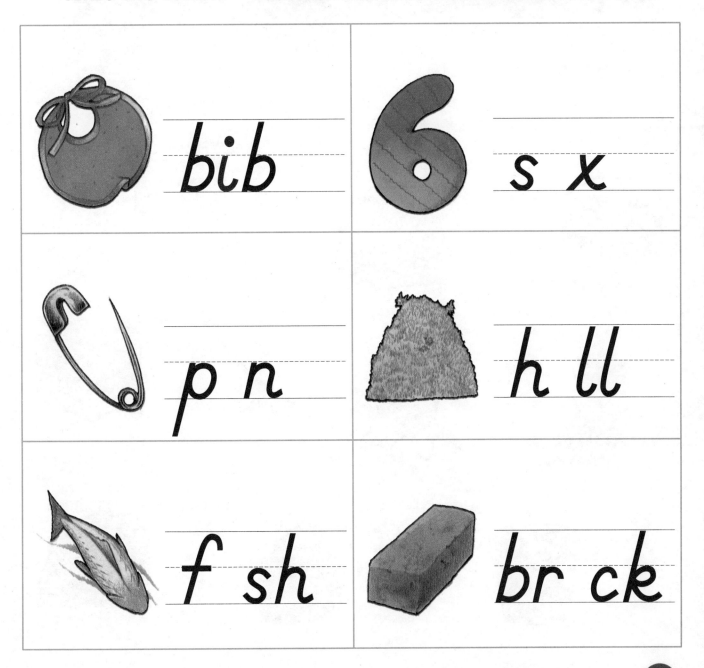

bib	s x
p n	h ll
f sh	br ck

13

The /o/ Sound

 PRONUNCIATION STRATEGY
Name the pictures.
Circle the ones
with the same
middle sound as

fox

 PRONUNCIATION STRATEGY
Name the pictures.
Match the middle sounds.

PRONUNCIATION STRATEGY
Name the picture. Listen for the /o/ sound. Write the letter o.

O

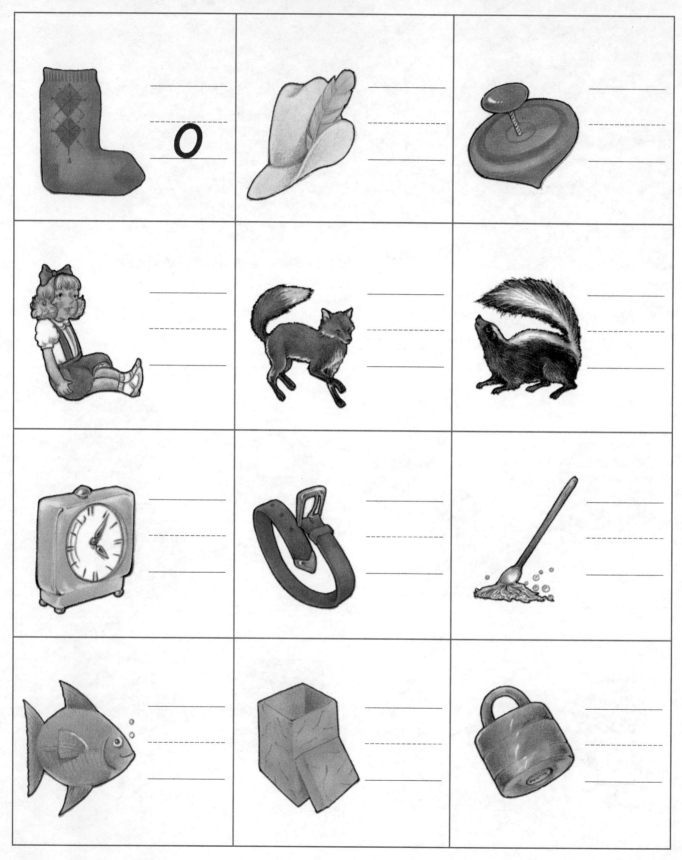

o

o o o

_p o t_

_r_ _ck_

_f_ _x_

_m_ _p_

_d_ _ll_

_l_ _ck_

14

The /u/ Sound

 PRONUNCIATION STRATEGY
Name the pictures.
Circle the ones
with the same
middle sound as

duck

 PRONUNCIATION STRATEGY
Name the pictures.
Match the middle sounds.

PRONUNCIATION STRATEGY
Name the picture. Listen for the /u/ sound. Write the letter *u*.

u

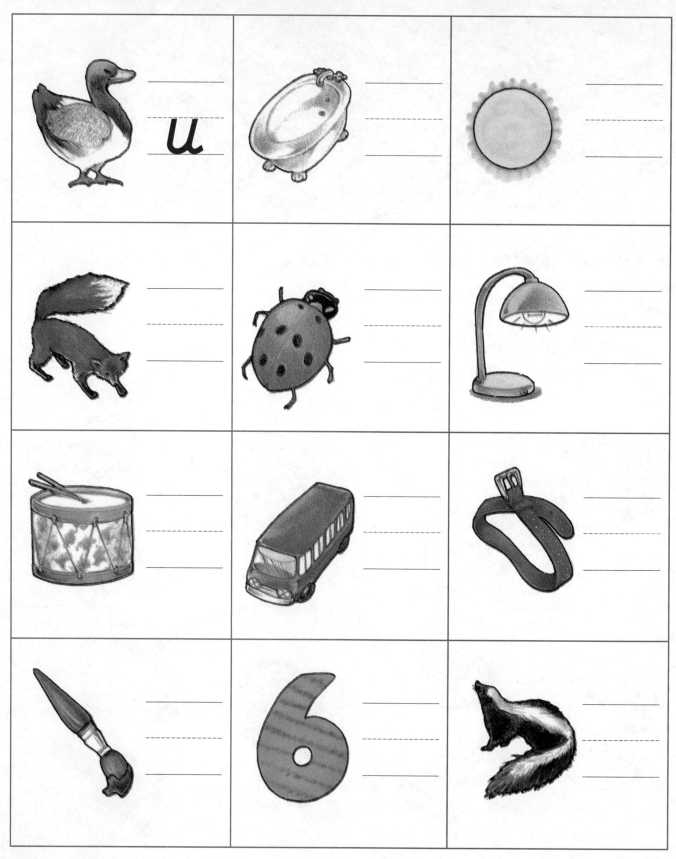

u

 PRONUNCIATION STRATEGY
Name the picture.
Write the letter.

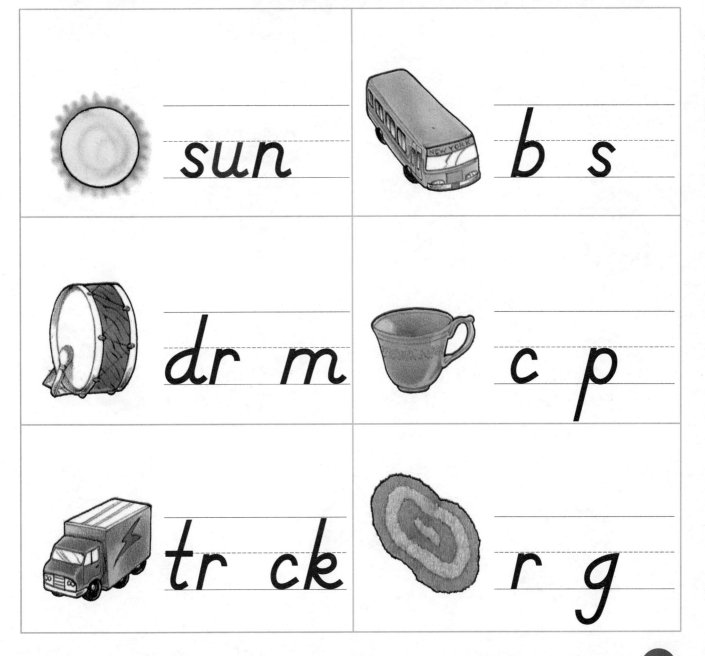

sun	b __ s
dr __ m	c __ p
tr __ ck	r __ g

15

The /e/ Sound

 PRONUNCIATION STRATEGY
Name the pictures.
Circle the ones
with the same
middle sound as

hen

 PRONUNCIATION STRATEGY
Name the pictures.
Match the middle sounds.

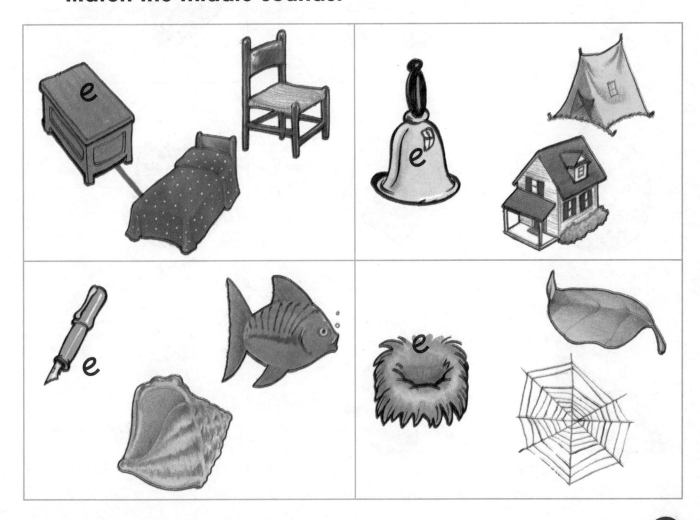

PRONUNCIATION STRATEGY
Name the picture. Listen for the /e/ sound. Write the letter e.

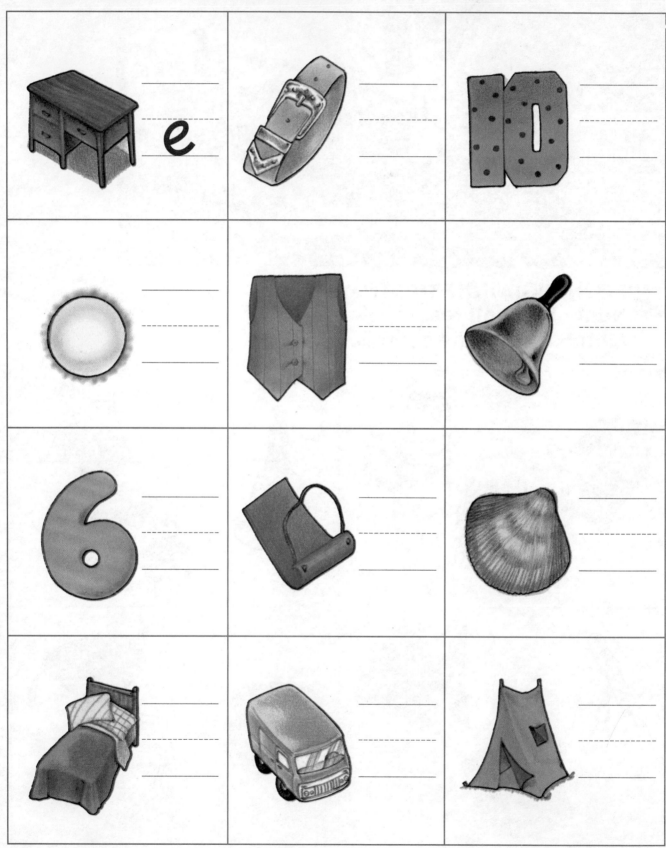

e

PRONUNCIATION STRATEGY
Name the picture.
Write the letter.

net	b _ d
t _ n	w _ b
v _ st	sl _ d

16 Review

for Lessons 11–15

PRONUNCIATION STRATEGY
Name the picture. Listen for the
middle sound. Circle the letter.

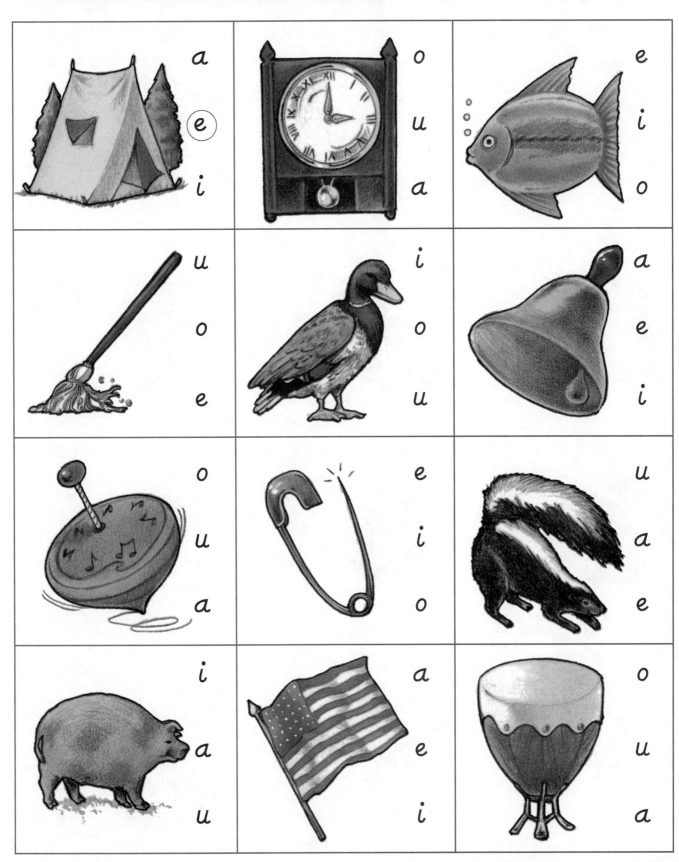

PRONUNCIATION STRATEGY
Name the picture. Listen for the
middle sound. Write the letter.

a e i o u

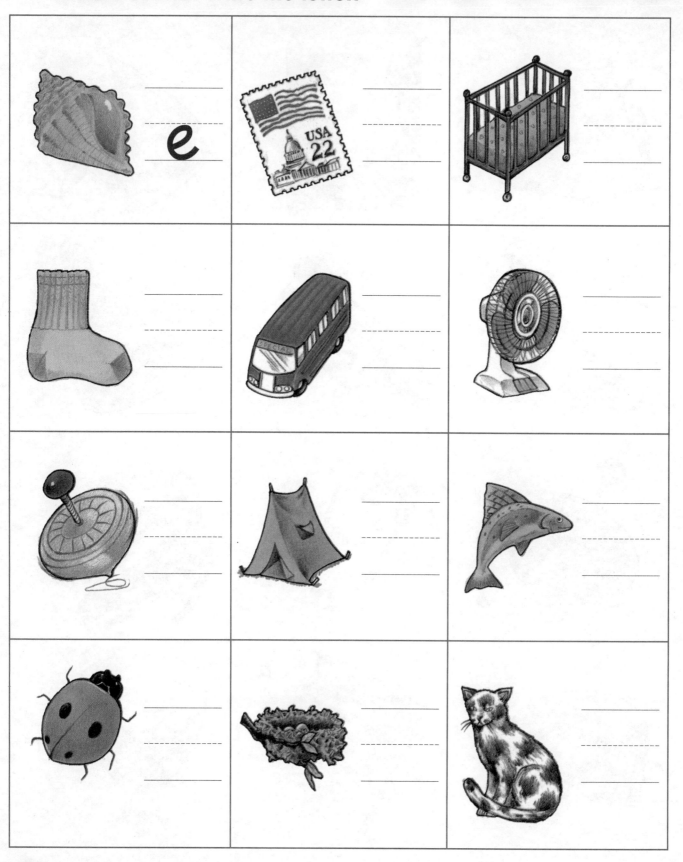

PRONUNCIATION STRATEGY
Name the picture. Listen for the
middle sound. Write the letter.

a e i o u

duck

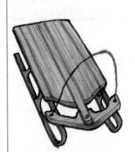

sl d

b t

m p

p g

m p

dr m

b ll

17 Words with the /a/ Sound

Spelling Focus—The /a/ sound can be spelled *a* as in *lamb*.

 PRONUNCIATION STRATEGY Write the Core Words. Say the words. Circle the letter that spells the /a/ sound.

 **Core Words**

1. ran

2. can

3. cat

4. sat

5. dad

6. bag

My Words

Core Word Sentences

He **ran** home.

Kick the tin **can.**

He got a **cat.**

She **sat** on the chair.

Is that your **dad?**

The **bag** is full.

1. _____

2. _____

3. _____

4. _____

5. _____

6. _____

MEANING STRATEGY Write the missing Core Words.

The Fast Cat

_____

The _____ jumped out of the

_____   _____

_____. My _____ and I

_____ after the cat. At last we

_____ down on the grass.

_____

That cat _____ run fast.

Core Words

1. ran
2. can
3. cat
4. sat
5. dad
6. bag

Challenge Words

am

and

fan

had

RHYMING STRATEGY Write the Core Word that rhymes with each word.

rag

1. _____

pan

2. _____

cat

3. _____

man

4. _____

bat

5. _____

sad

6. _____

CONSONANT-SUBSTITUTION STRATEGY Change or drop the first letter in each word to write a Challenge Word.

end

1. _____

tan

2. _____

bad

3. _____

jam

4. _____

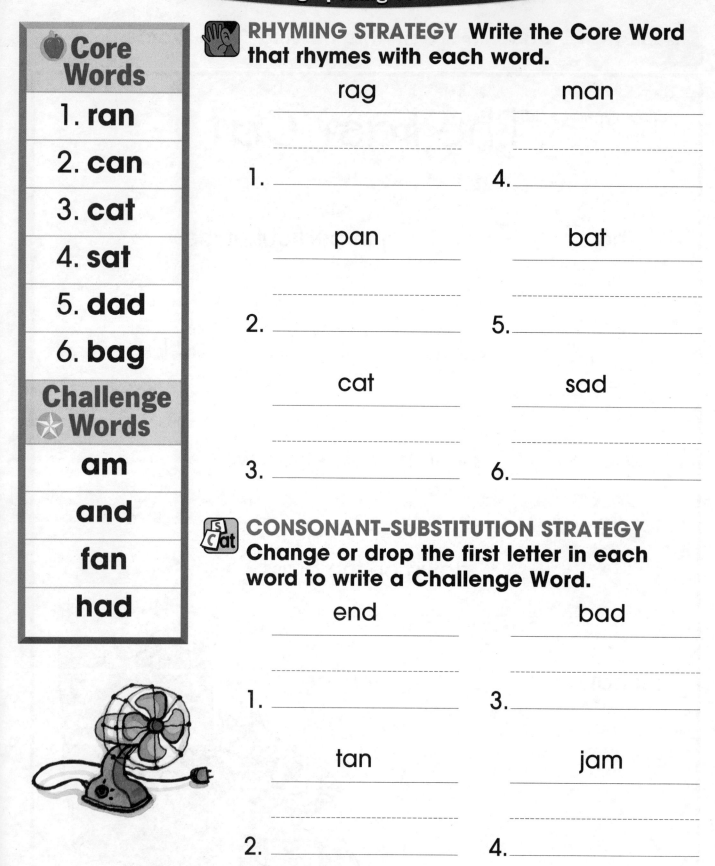

PROOFREADING STRATEGY Read the story. Find four misspelled Core Words. Circle them and write them correctly.

My dad runs. He kan run fast. He ran in the park. Then he sot down. He opened the bog. A small kat jumped out.

<table>
<tr><td>Proofreading
Marks</td></tr>
</table>

Proofreading Marks

⬭	misspelling
⊙	add a period
=	make a capital letter

1. _____   3. _____

2. _____   4. _____

MEANING STRATEGY Do you like to run? Write about a time you had to run fast. List and use four spelling words. Then check your work.

1. _____   3. _____

2. _____   4. _____

18 Words with the /i/ Sound

Spelling Focus—The /i/ sound can be spelled *i* as in p*i*g.

 PRONUNCIATION STRATEGY Write the Core Words. Say the words. Circle the letter that spells the /i/ sound.

 **Core Words**

1. *big*
2. *pig*
3. *did*
4. *in*
5. *win*
6. *sit*

My Words

Core Word Sentences

The lion is **big.**

He has a pet **pig.**

What **did** she say?

They are **in** the car.

The team has one **win.**

Please **sit** on the step.

1. _____

2. _____

3. _____

4. _____

5. _____

6. _____

MEANING STRATEGY Write the missing Core Words.

A First-Prize Hat

_____

My pet _____ won first prize

_____   _____

_____ a show. What _____ she

_____

_____ ? She won a _____ hat.

I hope she does not

_____

_____ on it!

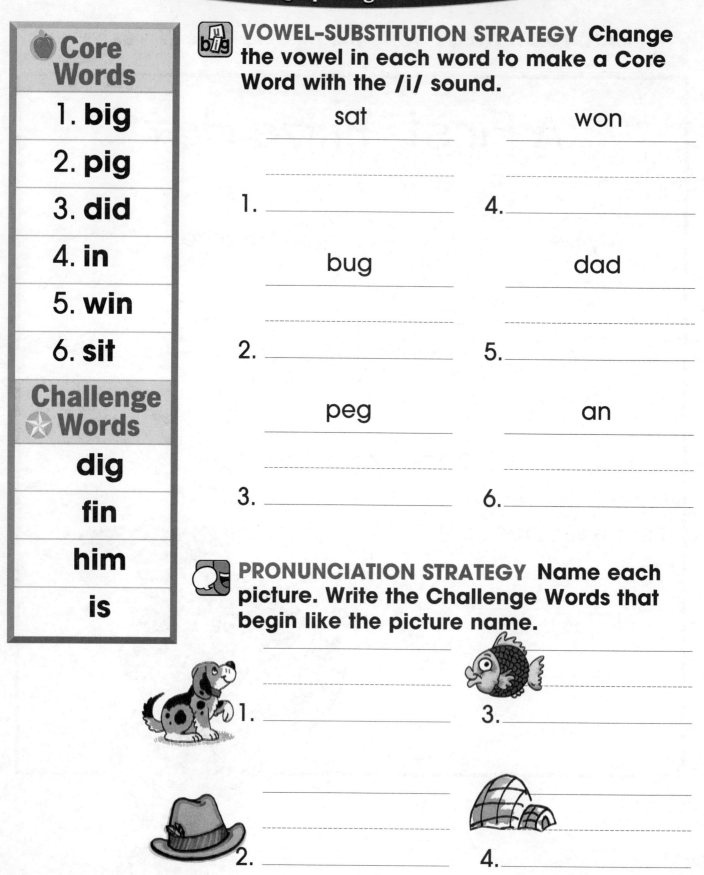

Core Words

1. **big**
2. **pig**
3. **did**
4. **in**
5. **win**
6. **sit**

Challenge Words

dig

fin

him

is

VOWEL-SUBSTITUTION STRATEGY Change the vowel in each word to make a Core Word with the /i/ sound.

sat

1. _____

bug

2. _____

peg

3. _____

won

4. _____

dad

5. _____

an

6. _____

PRONUNCIATION STRATEGY Name each picture. Write the Challenge Words that begin like the picture name.

1. _____

2. _____

3. _____

4. _____

PROOFREADING STRATEGY Read the story. Find four misspelled Core Words. Circle them and write them correctly.

I have a pet peg. She is not very bog. She can sat on my lap. She can fit un my bag.

1. _____   3. _____

2. _____   4. _____

MEANING STRATEGY Have you ever seen a pig or a picture of one? Write about what it looks like and what it does. List and use four spelling words. Then check your work.

1. _____   3. _____

2. _____   4. _____

19 Words with the /o/ Sound

Spelling Focus—The /o/ sound can be spelled *o* as in *fo̲x*.

 PRONUNCIATION STRATEGY Write the Core Words. Say the words. Circle the letter that spells the /o/ sound.

Core Words

1. hop
2. top
3. hot
4. not
5. box
6. fox

My Words

Core Word Sentences

I can **hop** on one foot.

The **top** spins fast.

The oven is **hot.**

Do **not** trip.

What is in the **box?**

The red **fox** runs fast.

1. _____

2. _____

3. _____

4. _____

5. _____

6. _____

MEANING STRATEGY Write the missing Core Words.

Fox in a Box

Look at the _____.

It is in the _____.

I hope it is not too _____.

The _____ of the box is open.

Can the fox _____ out?

I hope _____.

Core Words

1. hop
2. top
3. hot
4. not
5. box
6. fox

Challenge Words

got

mom

pop

pot

PRONUNCIATION STRATEGY Say the words. Figure out the missing vowels. Then write the Core Words.

f_x

t_p

1. _____

4. _____

h_p

b_x

2. _____

5. _____

h_t

n_t

3. _____

6. _____

VISUALIZATION STRATEGY Write the Challenge Words that each begin and end with the same letter.

1. _____

2. _____

RHYMING STRATEGY Write the Challenge Words that rhyme.

3. _____

4. _____

PROOFREADING STRATEGY Read the story. Find four misspelled Core Words. Circle them and write them correctly.

This fix is hat. He does nit like to run. He will jump and hup. Then he will go for a swim.

<table>
<tr><td>Proofreading Marks</td></tr>
</table>

Proofreading Marks
⬭ misspelling
⊙ add a period
= make a capital letter

1. _____   3. _____

2. _____   4. _____

 MEANING STRATEGY What if you could only hop like a rabbit or a frog? Write about how your life would change. List and use four spelling words. Then check your work.

1. _____   3. _____

2. _____   4. _____

20 Words with the /u/ Sound

Spelling Focus—The /u/ sound can be spelled *u* as in *tug*.

PRONUNCIATION STRATEGY Write the Core Words. Say the words. Circle the letter that spells the /u/ sound.

Core Words

1. hug
2. bug
3. but
4. nut
5. run
6. sun

My Words

Core Word Sentences

Give me a **hug!**

The **bug** flew away.

I am sad **but** not mad.

Do not eat that **nut.**

Can you **run** fast?

The **sun** is hot.

1. _____

2. _____

3. _____

4. _____

5. _____

6. _____

MEANING STRATEGY Write the missing Core Words.

My Pup

_____

My pup and I _____ in the

_____   _____

_____. My pup finds a _____,

_____

_____ it runs away. We sit under a

_____

_____ tree.

I give my pup

_____

a _____.

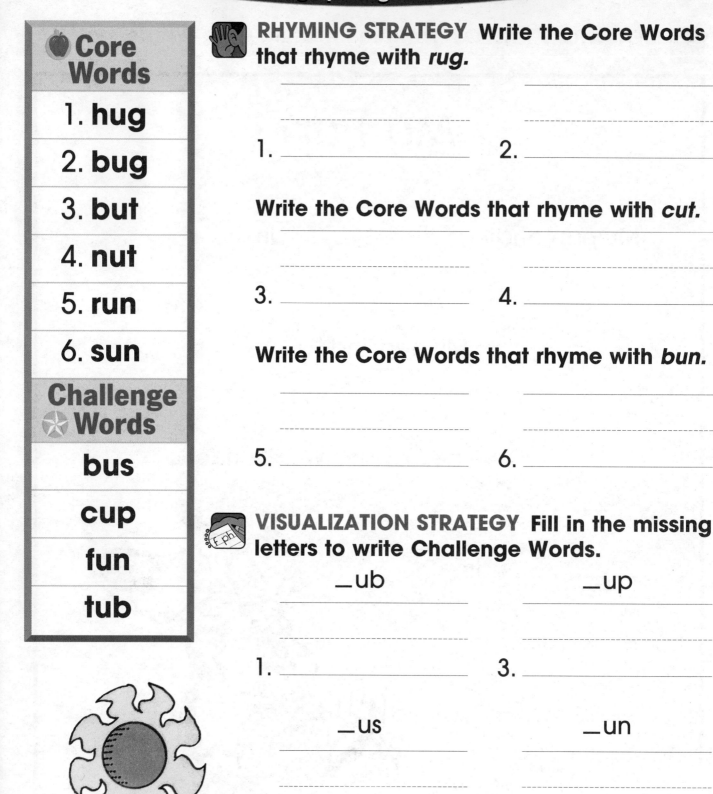

Core Words

1. hug
2. bug
3. but
4. nut
5. run
6. sun

Challenge Words

bus

cup

fun

tub

RHYMING STRATEGY Write the Core Words that rhyme with *rug*.

1. _____   2. _____

Write the Core Words that rhyme with *cut*.

3. _____   4. _____

Write the Core Words that rhyme with *bun*.

5. _____   6. _____

VISUALIZATION STRATEGY Fill in the missing letters to write Challenge Words.

_ub   _up

1. _____   3. _____

_us   _un

2. _____   4. _____

PROOFREADING STRATEGY Read the poem. Find four misspelled Core Words. Circle them and write them correctly.

I like to ran in the sunn.
I see things when I run.
Today I saw a beg.
When I got home, I got a hig.

Proofreading Marks

⬭ misspelling
⊙ add a period
= make a capital letter

1. _____   3. _____

2. _____   4. _____

MEANING STRATEGY Write about a pet you have or would like to have. What could you do together? List and use four spelling words. Then check your work.

1. _____   3. _____

2. _____   4. _____

21 Words with the /e/ Sound

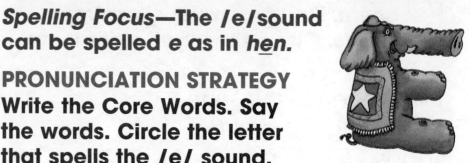

Spelling Focus—The /e/sound can be spelled *e* as in *h<u>e</u>n*.

PRONUNCIATION STRATEGY
Write the Core Words. Say the words. Circle the letter that spells the /e/ sound.

🍎 Core Words

1. get
2. net
3. pet
4. wet
5. hen
6. leg

My Words

Core Word Sentences

We all **get** a toy.

Fish are in the **net.**

You can **pet** the dog.

My feet got **wet.**

The **hen** laid an egg.

My **leg** hurts.

1. _____

2. _____

3. _____

4. _____

5. _____

6. _____

MEANING STRATEGY Write the missing Core Words.

A Wet Hen

_____   _____

How did you _____ so _____?

_____   _____

My _____ _____ ran

out in the rain. Her _____

was stuck in a _____.

 MEANING STRATEGY Write the Core Word that
fits each clue.

_____

1. A knee is part of this. _____

_____

2. This can be a dog or cat. _____

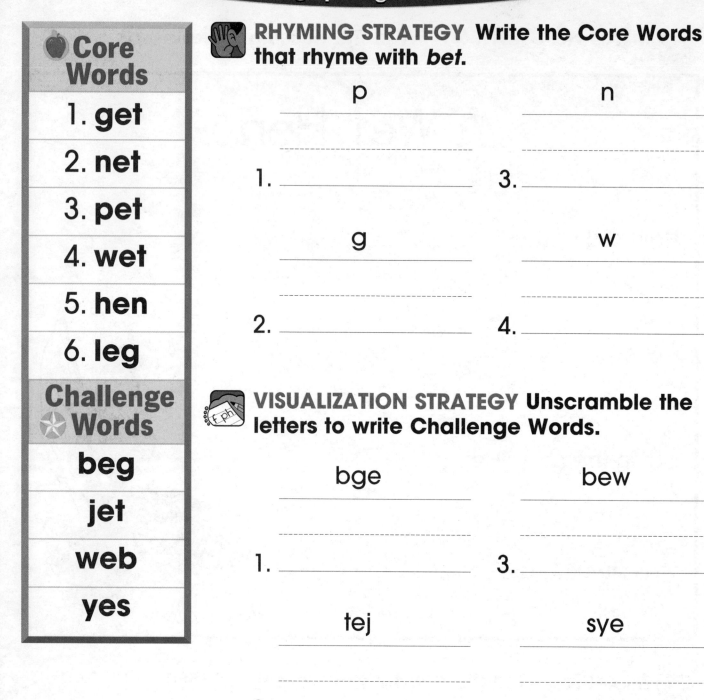

Core Words

🍎 **Core Words**

1. **get**
2. **net**
3. **pet**
4. **wet**
5. **hen**
6. **leg**

Challenge Words

⭐ **Challenge Words**

beg

jet

web

yes

RHYMING STRATEGY Write the Core Words that rhyme with *bet*.

p

1. _____

n

3. _____

g

2. _____

w

4. _____

VISUALIZATION STRATEGY Unscramble the letters to write Challenge Words.

bge

1. _____

bew

3. _____

tej

2. _____

sye

4. _____

PROOFREADING STRATEGY Read the story. Find four misspelled Core Words. Circle them and write them correctly.

Have you seen my hin? I will give her a bath. She will got wet. She will be a wot pat.

Proofreading Marks

⬭ misspelling

⊙ add a period

= make a capital letter

1. _____

2. _____

3. _____

4. _____

HENRIETTA

HENRIETTA

MEANING STRATEGY Write about what you like to do on a rainy day. List and use four spelling words. Then check your work.

1. _____

2. _____

3. _____

4. _____

22 Review *for Lessons 17–21*

 RHYMING STRATEGY Write the Core Words that rhyme with the picture name.

Lesson 17

ran

can

cat

sat

dad

bag

1. _____   2. _____

 MEANING STRATEGY Write the Core Word that completes the sentence.

3. My _____ is my father.

 RHYMING STRATEGY Write the Core Words that rhyme with the picture names.

Lesson 18

big

pig

did

in

win

sit

1. _____   2. _____

 VISUALIZATION STRATEGY Write the Core Words that begin like the picture names.

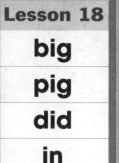 3. _____    4. _____

86 **Lesson 22 Review**

Review

Lesson 19
hop
top
hot
not
box
fox

RHYMING STRATEGY Write the Core Words that rhyme with the picture name.

1. _____

2. _____

MEANING STRATEGY Write the Core Word that fits the clue.

3. It is a container used to store things.

_____

Lesson 20

Lesson 20
hug
bug
but
nut
run
sun

RHYMING STRATEGY Write the Core Words that rhyme with the picture name.

1. _____

2. _____

RHYMING STRATEGY Write the Core Words that rhyme with this word.

3. bun _____

Review

Lesson 21

get
net
pet
wet
hen
leg

RHYMING STRATEGY Write two Core Words that rhyme with the picture name.

1. _____   2. _____

MEANING STRATEGY Write the Core Word that is an antonym, or opposite, of each word.

3. dry _____   4. give _____

Spelling Sounds

Write the different ways to spell these vowel sounds.

1. /a/ _____   4. /u/ _____

2. /i/ _____   5. /e/ _____

3. /o/ _____

Review

 PROOFREADING STRATEGY
**Read the sentences. Find three
misspelled Core Words. Circle
them and write them correctly.**

Proofreading Marks	
⬭	misspelling
═	make a capital letter
⊙	add a period

i have a pet henn.
The kat likes to chase her.
the foxe chases the cat.

1. _____   2. _____   3. _____

**Now find two words that should begin with a
capital letter. Underline each letter three
times to show it should be a capital letter.**

 MEANING STRATEGY Write about a
cat. Tell what it looks like and what
it does. List and use four spelling
words. Then check your work.

1. _____   3. _____

2. _____   4. _____

23 Words with *cl* and *fl*

Spelling Focus—The /cl/ sound can be spelled *cl*. The /fl/ sound can be spelled *fl*.

PRONUNCIATION STRATEGY
Write the Core Words spelled the following ways.

● **Core Words**

1. *clam*

2. *flag*

3. *flip*

4. *clap*

5. *flat*

6. *club*

My Words

Core Word Sentences

He ate a **clam.**

The **flag** was waving.

She did a **flip.**

I **clap** my hands.

He wore a **flat** hat.

I am in a **club.**

cl

1. _____

2. _____

3. _____

fl

1. _____

2. _____

3. _____

MEANING STRATEGY Write the missing Core Words.

A Clam in the Sand

Sue is in our beach _____. She

found a _____ in the sand. She tried to

_____ it over. It fell

with a loud _____.

 MEANING STRATEGY Write the Core Word that fits each clue.

1. You can wave me. _____

2. I am not round. _____

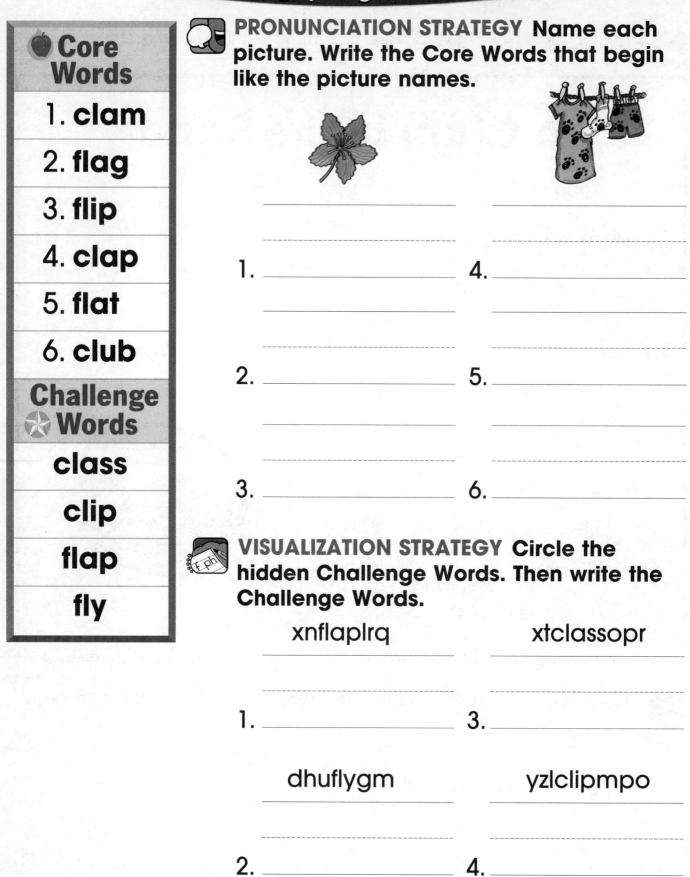

Building Spelling Vocabulary

Core Words

🍎 Core
   Words

1. **clam**
2. **flag**
3. **flip**
4. **clap**
5. **flat**
6. **club**

⭐ **Challenge
   Words**

class

clip

flap

fly

PRONUNCIATION STRATEGY Name each picture. Write the Core Words that begin like the picture names.

1. _____

2. _____

3. _____

4. _____

5. _____

6. _____

VISUALIZATION STRATEGY Circle the hidden Challenge Words. Then write the Challenge Words.

xnflaplrq

1. _____

dhuflygm

2. _____

xtclassopr

3. _____

yzlclipmpo

4. _____

PROOFREADING STRATEGY Read the story. Find four misspelled Core Words. Circle them and write them correctly.

Our clubb has a flate roof. We got a flagge to put on the roof. Please klap when you see the flag.

Proofreading Marks
⬭ misspelling
⊙ add a period
＝ make a capital letter

1. _____   3. _____

2. _____   4. _____

 MEANING STRATEGY Would you like to start a club? Write about a club for you and your friends. List and use four spelling words. Then check your work.

1. _____   3. _____

2. _____   4. _____

24 Words with *sn* and *st*

Spelling Focus—The /sn/ sound can be spelled *sn*. The /st/ sound can be spelled *st*.

 VISUALIZATION STRATEGY Write the Core Words spelled the following ways.

Core Words

1. step
2. snake
3. stay
4. stop
5. snug
6. snap

My Words

Core Word Sentences

Watch your **step**.

The **snake** crawls.

Will you **stay** home?

The rain will **stop**.

The hat was **snug**.

I **snap** my fingers.

sn

1. _____

2. _____

3. _____

st

1. _____

2. _____

3. _____

MEANING STRATEGY Write the missing Core Words.

A Snake on the Path

Ron heard a twig _____. He did not

_____ _____

_____ running. He had to _____

_____

over a _____ on the path.

_____

He did not _____ on the path.

He is home safe

_____

and _____.

SNAP!

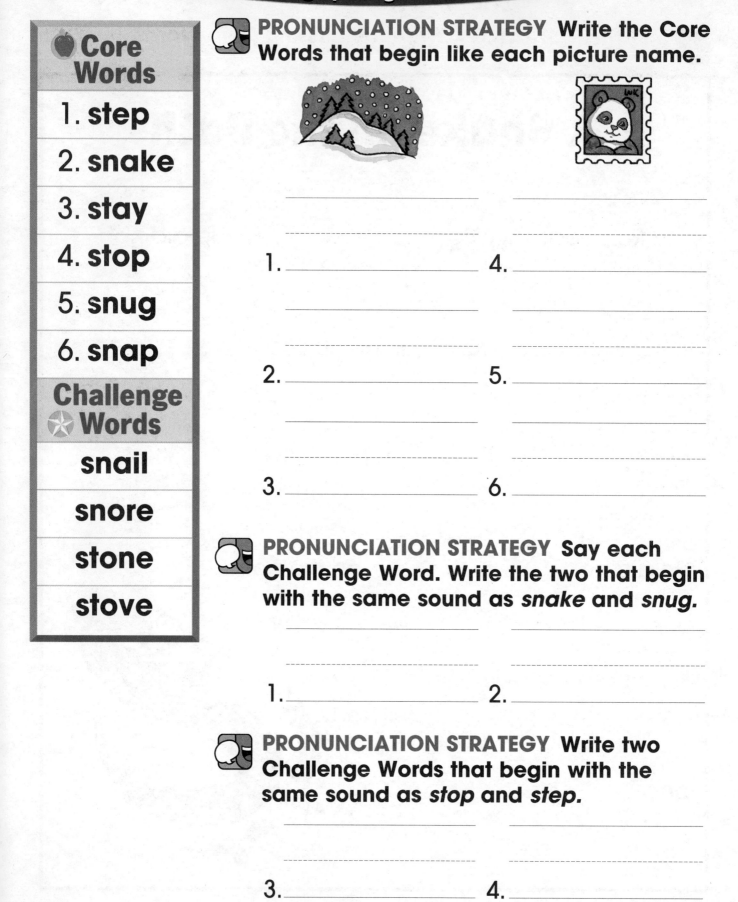

Core Words

1. **step**
2. **snake**
3. **stay**
4. **stop**
5. **snug**
6. **snap**

Challenge Words

snail

snore

stone

stove

PRONUNCIATION STRATEGY Write the Core Words that begin like each picture name.

1. _____

2. _____

3. _____

4. _____

5. _____

6. _____

PRONUNCIATION STRATEGY Say each Challenge Word. Write the two that begin with the same sound as *snake* and *snug.*

1. _____

2. _____

PRONUNCIATION STRATEGY Write two Challenge Words that begin with the same sound as *stop* and *step.*

3. _____

4. _____

PROOFREADING STRATEGY Read the story. Find four misspelled Core Words. Circle them and write them correctly.

The snaik and the snail had a race. The snale had to stopp when he got tired. He did not want to staye in the race.

Proofreading Marks

⬭	misspelling
⊙	add a period
=	make a capital letter

1. _____   3. _____

2. _____   4. _____

 MEANING STRATEGY What do you know about snakes? Write about what snakes are like. List and use four spelling words. Then check your work.

1. _____   3. _____

2. _____   4. _____

25 Words with *ch* and *th*

Spelling Focus—The /ch/ sound can be spelled *ch* as in <u>chipmunk</u>. The /th/ sound can be spelled *th* as in <u>the</u>.

PRONUNCIATION STRATEGY Say and write the Core Words with /ch/ and /th/ spelled the following ways.

🍎 Core Words

1. then
2. that
3. chat
4. chin
5. this
6. chop

My Words

Core Word Sentences

What did you do **then**?

I like **that** one.

Let's have a **chat**.

She hurt her **chin**.

Is **this** your desk?

Eat the lamb **chop**.

ch

1. _____

2. _____

3. _____

th

1. _____   2. _____

3. _____

MEANING STRATEGY Write the missing Core Words.

A Car That Sails

_____

Maria said, "I want a toy like _____

boat." Jack said, "I want one like _____

car." Their mother helped them _____ some

_____

wood. _____ they made a boat with wheels!

 MEANING STRATEGY Write the Core Word that fits each clue.

_____

1. I mean the same as _talk._   _____

2. I am part of your face.   _____

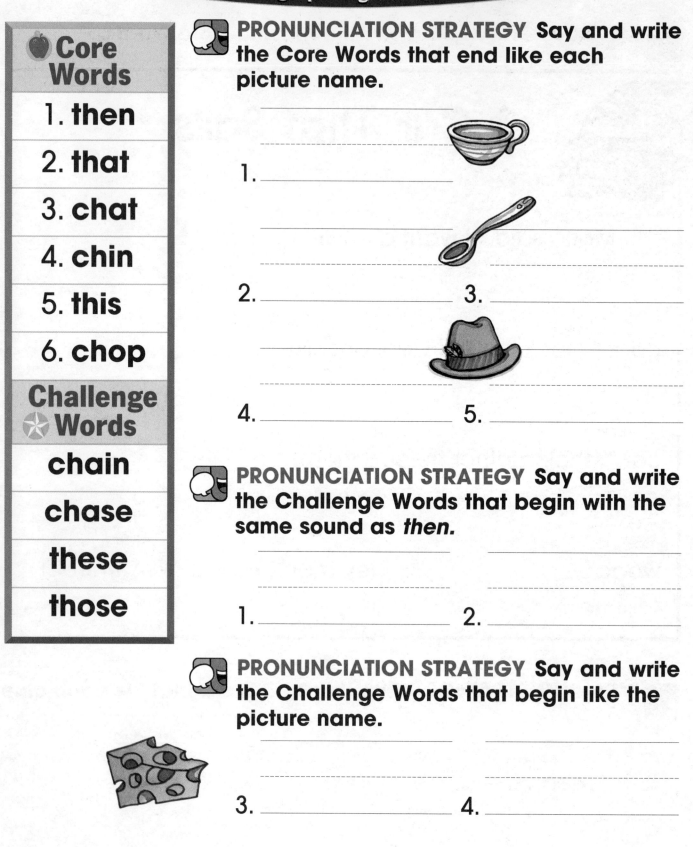

Core Words

1. then
2. that
3. chat
4. chin
5. this
6. chop

Challenge Words

chain

chase

these

those

PRONUNCIATION STRATEGY Say and write the Core Words that end like each picture name.

1. _____

2. _____   3. _____

4. _____   5. _____

PRONUNCIATION STRATEGY Say and write the Challenge Words that begin with the same sound as *then*.

1. _____   2. _____

PRONUNCIATION STRATEGY Say and write the Challenge Words that begin like the picture name.

3. _____   4. _____

PROOFREADING STRATEGY Read the story. Find four misspelled Core Words. Circle them and write them correctly.

Grandpa and I had a long chot. He said, "I planted thaat tree over there. I was only a boy than. Will you help me plant thiss new one?"

Proofreading Marks

⬭	misspelling
⊙	add a period
≡	make a capital letter

1. _____

2. _____

3. _____

4. _____

MEANING STRATEGY Do you have a favorite toy? Write about why you like it. List and use four spelling words. Then check your work.

1. _____

2. _____

3. _____

4. _____

26 Words with *wh* and *sh*

🍎 Core Words

1. *ship*
2. *when*
3. *shape*
4. *whale*
5. *shop*
6. *which*

My Words

Spelling Focus—The /hw/ sound can be spelled *wh* as in <u>whale</u>. The /sh/ sound can be spelled *sh* as in <u>shell</u>.

PRONUNCIATION STRATEGY Say and write the Core Words with /hw/ and /sh/ spelled the following ways.

Core Word Sentences

I will **ship** the box.

Call **when** you can.

It has a square **shape.**

I saw the **whale.**

The **shop** is open.

I know **which** way to go.

wh

1. _____

2. _____

3. _____

sh

1. _____

2. _____

3. _____

MEANING STRATEGY Write the missing Core Words.

The Toy Shop

The toy _____ is on

my street. A bell rings _____ you go in.

There is a sailing _____ and a gray

_____. I like the _____ of it. Do

you know _____ one it is?

Core Words

1. **ship**
2. **when**
3. **shape**
4. **whale**
5. **shop**
6. **which**

Challenge Words

shark

shell

where

why

RHYMING STRATEGY Write the Core Words that rhyme with these words.

switch

hop

1. _____   4. _____

trip

sale

2. _____   5. _____

then

tape

3. _____   6. _____

PRONUNCIATION STRATEGY Say and write the Challenge Words that begin like each picture name.

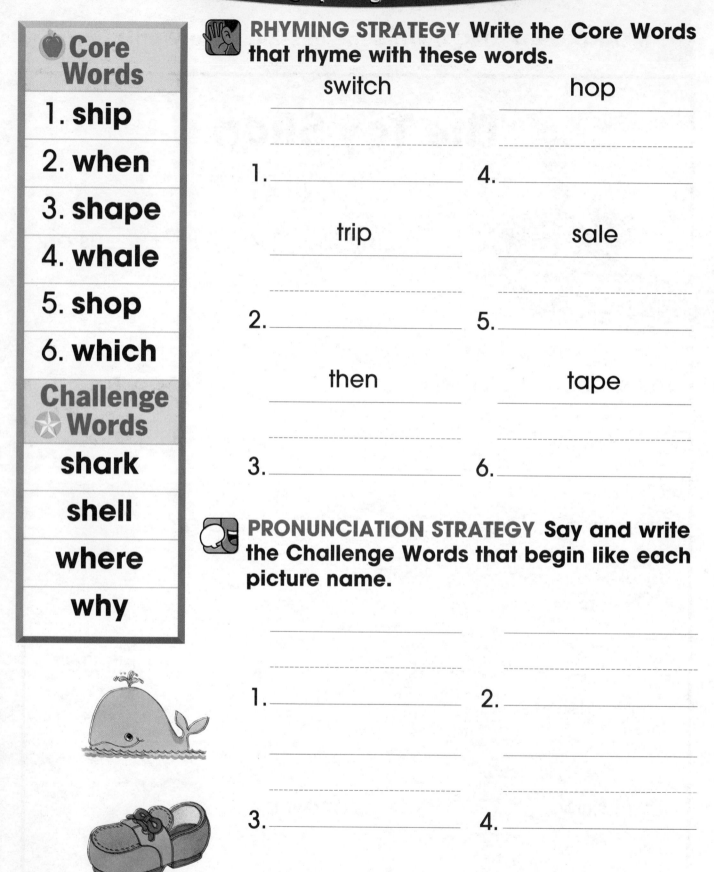

1. _____   2. _____

3. _____   4. _____

PROOFREADING STRATEGY Read the story. Find four misspelled Core Words. Circle them and write them correctly.

Proofreading Marks
⬭ misspelling
⊙ add a period
＝ make a capital letter

I saw a pretty shippe in the shopp. It was next to a toy whail. Do you know wich one you would like to have?

1. _____   3. _____

2. _____   4. _____

MEANING STRATEGY
What do you know about whales? Write about whales. List and use four spelling words. Then check your work.

1. _____   3. _____

2. _____   4. _____

27 Review for Lessons 23–26

Lesson 23

Lesson 23
clam
flag
flip
clap
flat
club

PRONUNCIATION STRATEGY Say and write two Core Words that begin like the picture name.

1. _____

2. _____

MEANING STRATEGY Write the Core Word that fits each meaning.

3. turn over

4. level and smooth

Lesson 24

Lesson 24
step
snake
stay
stop
snug
snap

PRONUNCIATION STRATEGY Say and write two Core Words that begin like the picture name.

1. _____

2. _____

VISUALIZATION STRATEGY Fill in the missing letters to write Core Words.

3. _ _ay _____

4. _ _op _____

Review

Lesson 25
then
that
chat
chin
this
chop

PRONUNCIATION STRATEGY Say and write two Core Words that begin like the picture name.

1. _____   2. _____

MEANING STRATEGY Write the Core Word that completes the sentence.

3. My mother will _____ wood.

Lesson 26
ship
when
shape
whale
shop
which

PRONUNCIATION STRATEGY Say and write two Core Words that begin like the picture name.

1. _____   2. _____

VISUALIZATION STRATEGY Write *sh* or *wh* at the beginning of each word to make a Core Word.

3. _____ ip   4. _____ ale

Review

Write the different ways to spell these sounds. Then write one Core Word from pages 106–107 for each sound.

1. /cl/ and /fl/

_____   _____

_____   _____

_____   _____

_____   _____

2. /sn/ and /st/

_____   _____

_____   _____

_____   _____

_____   _____

3. /ch/ and /th/

_____   _____

_____   _____

_____   _____

_____   _____

Review

PROOFREADING STRATEGY Read the story. Find three misspelled Core Words. Circle them and write them correctly.

i saw a whail. I told my clubb about it. i hope the whale will sta for a while.

Proofreading Marks	
⬭	misspelling
＝	make a capital letter
⊙	add a period

1. _____

2. _____

3. _____

Now find two words that should begin with a capital letter. Underline each letter three times to show it should be a capital letter.

MEANING STRATEGY What animals do you know about? Write about some animals that you like. List and use four spelling words. Then check your work.

1. _____

2. _____

3. _____

4. _____

28 The /ā/ Sound

Core Words

1. may
2. bake
3. name
4. day
5. gave
6. way

My Words

Spelling Focus—The /ā/ sound can be spelled *a—e* as in **make** and *—ay* as in **say**.

VISUALIZATION STRATEGY
Write the Core Words spelled the following ways.

a_e

Core Word Sentences

He **may** not need it.

Did you **bake** the cake?

Her **name** is Holly.

What **day** can you go?

I **gave** her a pen.

Do it that **way.**

1. _____

2. _____

3. _____

 **ay**

1. _____

2. _____

3. _____

MEANING STRATEGY Write the missing Core Words.

Baking Bread

My uncle's _____ is Dave.

He likes to _____ bread.

One _____ we made some.

Uncle Dave showed me the _____ to mix

the dough. Then he _____ me a turn. When

we were done, my parents asked, "_____

we have some?"

Core Words

1. **may**
2. **bake**
3. **name**
4. **day**
5. **gave**
6. **way**

Challenge Words

came

clay

play

take

 VISUALIZATION STRATEGY Fill in the missing letters to write the Core Words.

m_y

g_v_

1. _____

4. _____

n_m_

d_y

2. _____

5. _____

b_k_

w_y

3. _____

6. _____

 RHYMING STRATEGY Write the Challenge Words that rhyme with these words.

same

make

1. _____

2. _____

gray

3. _____

4. _____

PROOFREADING STRATEGY Read the story. Find four misspelled Core Words. Circle them and write them correctly.

My mom gaive me a book. It was about how to bak bread. I maid the bread by myself. When it was done, we ait it all!

1. _____

2. _____

3. _____

4. _____

MEANING STRATEGY Do you like to bake? Write about something fun you would like to make. List and use four spelling words. Then check your work.

1. _____

2. _____

3. _____

4. _____

29 The /ī/ Sound

Spelling Focus—The /ī/ sound can be spelled i__e as in _side_.

 PRONUNCIATION STRATEGY Say and write the Core Words. Circle the letters that spell the /ī/ sound.

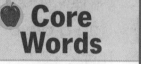 **Core Words**

1. hide
2. ride
3. bike
4. like
5. time
6. kite

My Words

Core Word Sentences

Mom will **hide** cookies.

He took a car **ride.**

I have a red **bike.**

We **like** school!

What **time** is it?

Can you fly a **kite?**

1. _____

2. _____

3. _____

4. _____

5. _____

6. _____

MEANING STRATEGY Write the missing Core Words.

At the Park

_____   _____

I _____ to _____

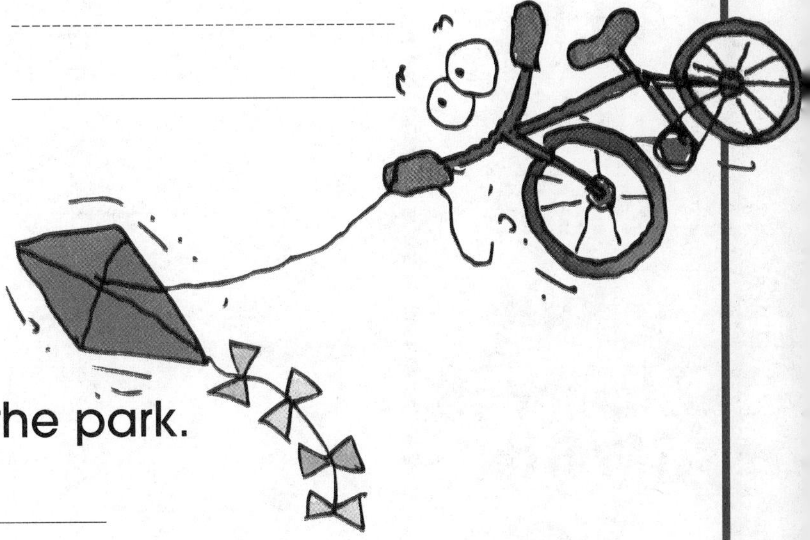

_____

my _____ in the park.

_____

Sometimes I _____ it behind a bush.

_____

Then I fly my _____. I have a good

_____

_____.

Core Words

1. hide
2. ride
3. bike
4. like
5. time
6. kite

Challenge Words

dime

fine

mine

size

 RHYMING STRATEGY Write the Core Words that rhyme with these words.

hike

1._____

2._____

bite

3._____

stride

4._____

5._____

lime

6._____

 VISUALIZATION STRATEGY Unscramble these letters to write the Challenge Words. Circle the letters that spell the /ī/ sound.

nfie

1._____

ezis

2._____

enmi

3._____

idme

4._____

PROOFREADING STRATEGY Read the story. Find four misspelled Core Words. Circle them and write them correctly.

Dad has a big blue kight. We lik to fly it at the park. I also like to ride my bikke.We always have a good tim.

Proofreading Marks	
⬭	misspelling
⊙	add a period
＝	make a capital letter

1. _____

2. _____

3. _____

4. _____

MEANING STRATEGY Have you ever seen a kite fly? Write about a kite. List and use four spelling words. Then check your work.

1. _____

2. _____

3. _____

4. _____

30 The /ō/ Sound

Spelling Focus—The /ō/ sound can be spelled *o* as in <u>so</u> and *o—e* as in <u>robe</u>.

VISUALIZATION STRATEGY
Write the Core Words spelled the following ways.

Core Words

1. go
2. no
3. note
4. home
5. bone
6. rope

My Words

Core Word Sentences

I want to **go** play.

We have **no** clay.

He wrote a **note.**

My **home** is nearby.

The dog found a **bone.**

The **rope** was long.

o

1. _____

2. _____

o_e

1. _____

2. _____

3. _____

4. _____

MEANING STRATEGY Write the missing Core Words.

Visiting Pat

I tied a _____ to the wagon. My dog

Rover put his _____ in the wagon. We

decided to _____ see Pat. I asked if she

was home. Her mother said "_____." So I left

a _____. Then I took Rover

🍎 **Core Words**

1. **go**
2. **no**
3. **note**
4. **home**
5. **bone**
6. **rope**

Challenge ⭐ Words

hope

joke

pole

rode

RHYMING STRATEGY Write the Core Word that rhymes with each picture name.

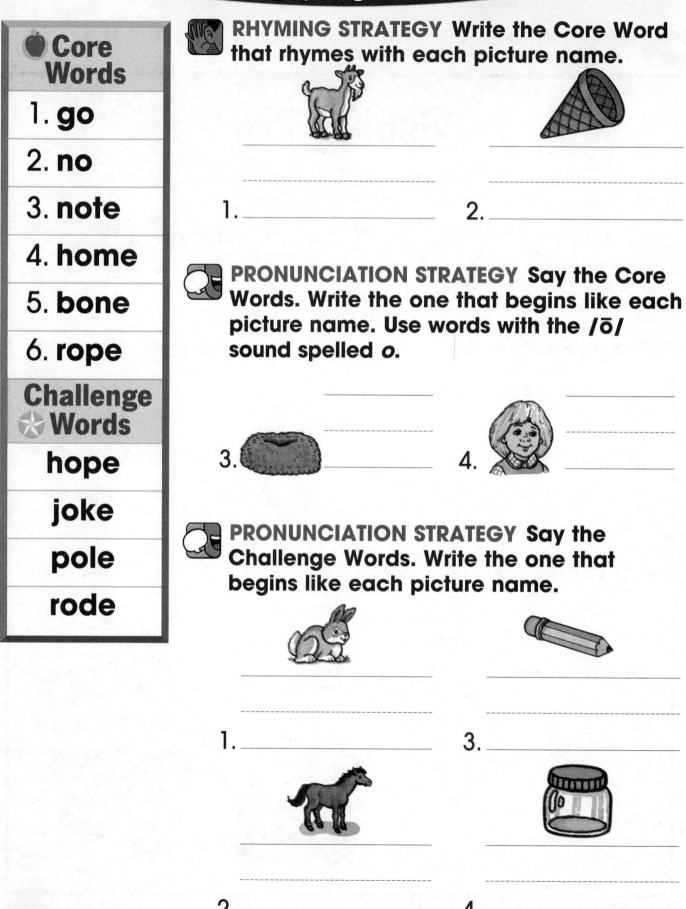

1. _____

2. _____

PRONUNCIATION STRATEGY Say the Core Words. Write the one that begins like each picture name. Use words with the /ō/ sound spelled *o.*

3. _____

4. _____

PRONUNCIATION STRATEGY Say the Challenge Words. Write the one that begins like each picture name.

1. _____

3. _____

2. _____

4. _____

PROOFREADING STRATEGY Read the story. Find four misspelled Core Words. Circle them and write them correctly.

I came hom from school. Rover wanted to gow for a walk. He wanted to find his bon. There were noh bones in the house.

Proofreading Marks

◯ misspelling

⊙ add a period

= make a capital letter

1. _____

2. _____

3. _____

4. _____

MEANING STRATEGY What do you like to do with your friends? Write about a good time you had with friends. Use four of your spelling words. Then check your work.

1. _____

2. _____

3. _____

4. _____

31 The /ē/ Sound

 **Core Words**

1. he

2. me

3. bee

4. see

5. seed

6. weed

My Words

_____

_____

_____

_____

Spelling Focus—The /ē/ sound can be spelled *e* as in *me* and *ee* as in *tree*.

VISUALIZATION STRATEGY Write the Core Words spelled the following ways.

Core Word Sentences

When will **he** come?

Will you go with **me?**

The **bee** stung her.

Did you **see** the movie?

She planted a **seed.**

Please **weed** the garden.

ee

1. _____

2. _____

3. _____

4. _____

e

1. _____

2. _____

MEANING STRATEGY **Write the missing Core Words.**

A Bee Sting

_____

_____

Dad gave _____ an apple

_____   _____

_____. Then _____ pulled

_____   _____

up a _____. But he did not _____

_____

_____

the _____. Ouch!

Core Words

1. **he**
2. **me**
3. **bee**
4. **see**
5. **seed**
6. **weed**

Challenge Words

feel

feet

jeep

she

MEANING STRATEGY Fill in the missing letters. Write the Core Words.

m _

1. _____

h _

2. _____

b _ _

3. _____

w _ _ d

4. _____

s _ _

5. _____

s _ _ d

6. _____

PRONUNCIATION STRATEGY Match the word parts to make Challenge Words. Write the Challenge Words.

sh   eet
j   eel
f   e
f   eep

1. _____

2. _____

3. _____

4. _____

PROOFREADING STRATEGY Read the story. Find four misspelled Core Words. Circle them and write them correctly.

I went to sea the garden. I saw a bea near a weede. But he didn't see mee!

Proofreading Marks

⬭ misspelling

⊙ add a period

= make a capital letter

1. _____

2. _____

3. _____

4. _____

MEANING STRATEGY Do you like fruit? Write about the fruit you like. Tell what it looks like and how it tastes. List and use four spelling words. Then check your work.

1. _____

2. _____

3. _____

4. _____

32 Review for Lessons 28–31

Lesson 28

may
bake
name
day
gave
way

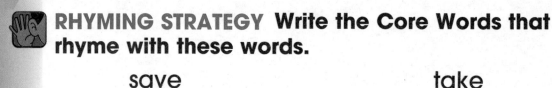

RHYMING STRATEGY Write two Core Words that rhyme with the word *say*.

1. _____   2. _____

RHYMING STRATEGY Write the Core Words that rhyme with these words.

save   take

3. _____   4. _____

Lesson 29

Lesson 29

hide
ride
bike
like
time
kite

RHYMING STRATEGY Write two Core Words that rhyme with *slide*.

1. _____   2. _____

VISUALIZATION STRATEGY Fill in the missing letter in each Core Word.

ki_e   ti_e

3. _____   4. _____

Review

Lesson 30
go
no
note
home
bone
rope

RHYMING STRATEGY Write two Core Words that rhyme with the word *crow.*

1. _____ 2. _____

MEANING STRATEGY Write the Core Word that fits the clue.

3. A skeleton is made of this.

_____

_____

Lesson 31

Lesson 31
he
me
bee
see
seed
weed

RHYMING STRATEGY Write two Core Words that rhyme with the word *deed.*

1. _____ 2. _____

VISUALIZATION STRATEGY Fill in the missing letter to write each Core Word.

3. h_ _____ 4. b_e _____

Review

Write the different ways to spell these vowel sounds. Then choose one Core Word from pages 126–127 for each vowel sound.

1. ā

3. ō

2. ī

4. ē

Review

![] **PROOFREADING STRATEGY** Read
the story. Find three misspelled
Core Words. Circle them and
write them correctly.

My nam is Stan. I carry my
hom on my back. It keeps
mee dry.

Proofreading Marks	
⬭	misspelling
═	make a capital letter
⊙	add a period

1. _____ 2. _____ 3. _____

**Now find two sentences that should end
with a period. Use the correct proofreading
mark to show where the periods should be.**

**MEANING STRATEGY What do you think
a snail does all day in the garden?
Write about a snail. List and use four
spelling words. Then check your work.**

1. _____

2. _____

3. _____

4. _____

33 Words You Use a Lot

Core Words

1. all
2. are
3. I
4. you
5. said
6. the

My Words

Spelling Focus—Some words are not spelled the way they sound. You must remember the spelling.

PRONUNCIATION STRATEGY Say and write the Core Words. Write the ones that fit the following groups. Remember that **y** is considered a consonant when it begins a word.

begin with consonants

Core Word Sentences

Give the game your **all.**

They **are** not at home.

Should **I** call you?

Do **you** like to sing?

She **said** it was fun.

We went to **the** movies.

1. _____

2. _____

3. _____

begin with vowels

1. _____

2. _____

3. _____

MEANING STRATEGY Write the missing Core Words.

A Zoo Trip

_____

- -

Our class went to _____ zoo.

_____

- - - - - - - - - - - -

" _____ am glad to see

_____   _____

- - - - - - - - - - -   - - - - - - - - - - -

_____ , " _____ the man.

_____

- - - - - - - - - - - - - - -

"Where _____ you going?"

"We are going to see

_____

- - - - - - - - - - - - - - -

_____ the animals," we said.

Core Words

1. all
2. are
3. I
4. you
5. said
6. the

Challenge Words

here
has
need
was

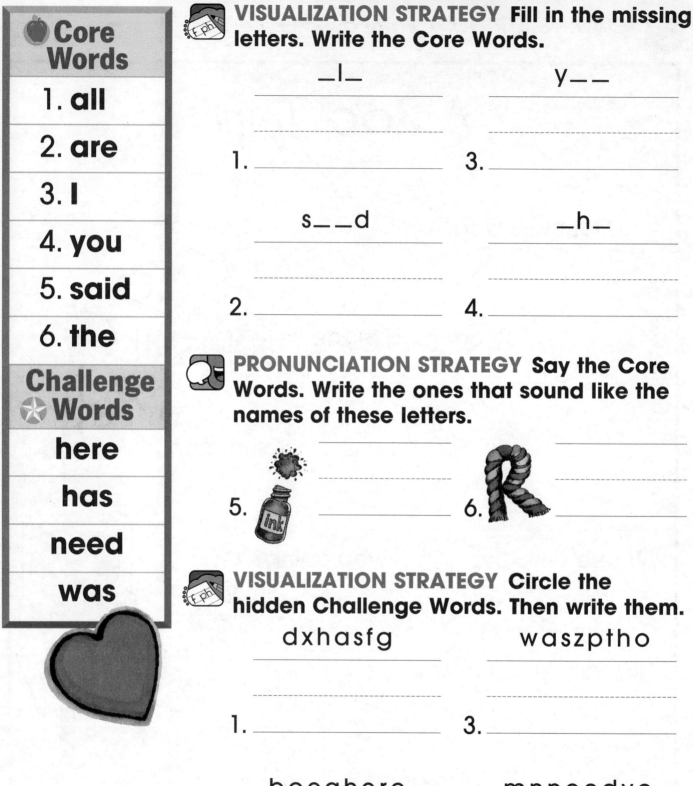

VISUALIZATION STRATEGY Fill in the missing letters. Write the Core Words.

_l_

y_ _

1. _____

3. _____

s_ _d

_h_

2. _____

4. _____

PRONUNCIATION STRATEGY Say the Core Words. Write the ones that sound like the names of these letters.

5. _____

6. _____

VISUALIZATION STRATEGY Circle the hidden Challenge Words. Then write them.

dxhasfg

waszptho

1. _____

3. _____

bocqhere

mnneedvc

2. _____

4. _____

PROOFREADING STRATEGY Read the sentences. Find four misspelled Core Words. Circle them and write them correctly.

"Look at oll the flags," sed Dick.
"Can yu name them?" asked Ann.
"There ar too many," I said.

Proofreading Marks

⬭ misspelling

⊙ add a period

= make a capital letter

1. _____   3. _____

2. _____   4. _____

MEANING STRATEGY Which animals do you like best? Write about animals you might see in a zoo. Use four of your spelling words. Then check your work.

I LIKE TO SWIM
I HAVE STRONG TEETH

1. _____   3. _____

2. _____   4. _____

34 More Words You Use a Lot

Spelling Focus—These words are not spelled the way they sound. You must remember the spelling.

PRONUNCIATION STRATEGY Say the Core Words. Write the ones that fit the following groups. Remember that *y* is considered a vowel when it is paired with *e*.

Core Words

1. come
2. do
3. want
4. have
5. her
6. they

My Words

Core Word Sentences

Can you **come** out to play?

What **do** you like?

I **want** a brother.

They **have** a new boat.

I want **her** to help.

Where do **they** live?

end with vowels

1. _____

2. _____

3. _____

4. _____

end with consonants

1. _____

2. _____

MEANING STRATEGY Write the missing Core Words.

Animal Parade

_____

Sue ran up to _____ sister.

_____

"I _____ to see the animals.

_____   _____

_____ we _____ to feed them?"

_____

"When are _____

coming?" "Here they

_____

_____ now!"

🍎 **Core Words**

1. **come**
2. **do**
3. **want**
4. **have**
5. **her**
6. **they**

Challenge Words

for

from

my

some

VISUALIZATION STRATEGY Change one letter in each word to make a Core Word.

them

1. _____

cone

2. _____

hem

3. _____

to

4. _____

hare

5. _____

went

6. _____

PRONUNCIATION STRATEGY Name each picture. Write the Challenge Words that begin like each picture name.

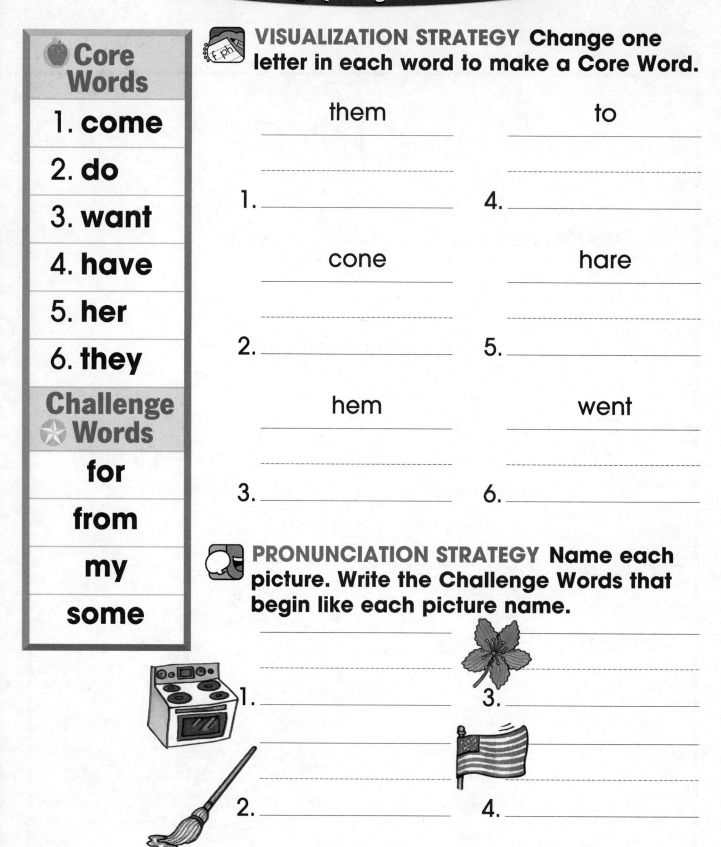

1. _____

2. _____

3. _____

4. _____

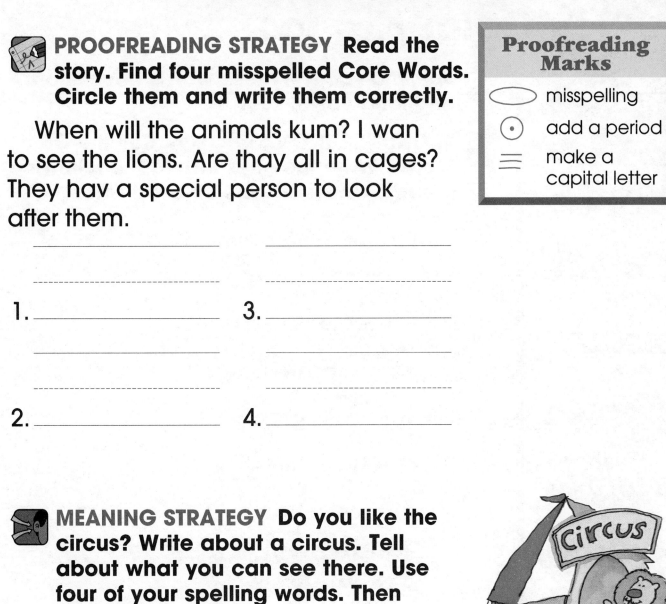

PROOFREADING STRATEGY Read the story. Find four misspelled Core Words. Circle them and write them correctly.

When will the animals kum? I wan to see the lions. Are thay all in cages? They hav a special person to look after them.

Proofreading Marks

⬭ misspelling

⊙ add a period

= make a capital letter

1. _____   3. _____

2. _____   4. _____

MEANING STRATEGY Do you like the circus? Write about a circus. Tell about what you can see there. Use four of your spelling words. Then check your work.

Circus

1. _____   3. _____

2. _____   4. _____

35 Color Names

Core Words

1. red
2. black
3. pink
4. green
5. white
6. yellow

My Words

Spelling Focus—These words have short and long vowel sounds.

PRONUNCIATION STRATEGY Say the Core Words. Write the ones that fit the following groups. One word will be used twice.

Core Word Sentences

She ate a **red** apple.

He saw a **black** cat.

She wore a **pink** dress.

The tomato is **green.**

I have **white** shells.

The corn is **yellow.**

short vowel sounds

1. _____

2. _____

3. _____

4. _____

long vowel sounds

1. _____

2. _____

3. _____

MEANING STRATEGY Look at the picture. Write the missing Core Words.

A Pretty Picture

_____

I painted a picture of a _____ cloud.

_____   _____

I mixed _____ and _____ to

_____

make pink. I added a _____ sun and

_____

some _____ grass.

_____

Then I drew a _____ bird.

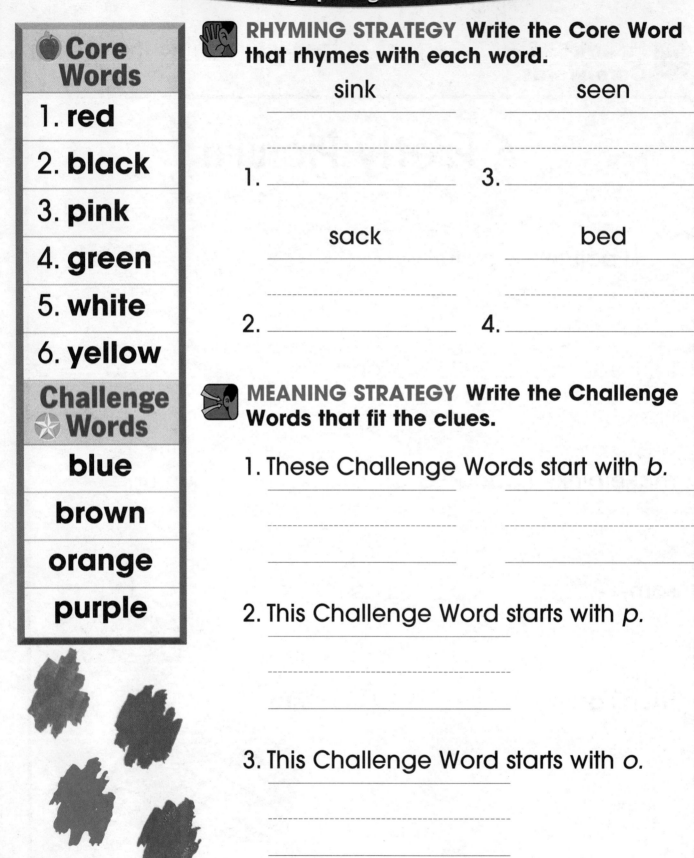

🍎 **Core Words**

1. **red**
2. **black**
3. **pink**
4. **green**
5. **white**
6. **yellow**

⭐ **Challenge Words**

blue

brown

orange

purple

RHYMING STRATEGY Write the Core Word that rhymes with each word.

sink

1. _____

seen

3. _____

sack

2. _____

bed

4. _____

MEANING STRATEGY Write the Challenge Words that fit the clues.

1. These Challenge Words start with *b.*

_____

_____

2. This Challenge Word starts with *p.*

_____

3. This Challenge Word starts with *o.*

_____

PROOFREADING STRATEGY Read the story. Find four misspelled Core Words. Circle them and write them correctly.

My dress is redd and black. Your shirt is yello. We both have grene eyes. We live in a wite house.

1. _____   3. _____

2. _____   4. _____

MEANING STRATEGY Do you like flowers? Write about flowers you like. Tell about how they look and smell. Use four of your spelling words. Then check your work.

1. _____   3. _____

2. _____   4. _____

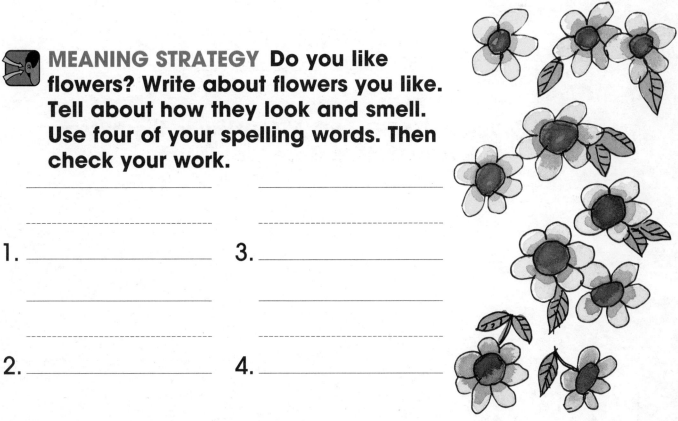

36 Review for Lessons 33–35

Lesson 33

all
are
I
you
said
the

PRONUNCIATION STRATEGY Write two Core Words that have the same beginning letter as the picture name.

1. _____ 2. _____

MEANING STRATEGY Write the Core Word that goes with each group of words.

3. you, he, _____

4. says, saying, _____

VISUALIZATION STRATEGY Fill in the missing letters to write a Core Word.

t_e   a_e

5. _____   7. _____

_ou   _ll

6. _____   8. _____

Review

Lesson 34
come
do
want
have
her
they

PRONUNCIATION STRATEGY Say the Core Words. Write the two that have the same beginning sound as the picture name.

1. _____   2. _____

MEANING STRATEGY Write the Core Word that completes each sentence.

3. I will _____ my chores today.

4. I think that _____ will come.

VISUALIZATION STRATEGY Write the Core Word that begins like each picture name.

5. _____

6. _____

Review

Lesson 35

Lesson 35
red
black
pink
green
white
yellow

PRONUNCIATION STRATEGY Say the Core Words. Write the ones that have the same vowel sound as the picture name.

1. _____

2. _____

MEANING STRATEGY Write the Core Word that completes each sentence.

3. A bee has _____ and

yellow stripes.

4. An egg can be brown or _____.

RHYMING STRATEGY Write the Core Word that rhymes with each word.

seen

sink

5. _____

6. _____

Review

 PROOFREADING STRATEGY Read the story. Find three misspelled Core Words. Circle them and write them correctly.

Proofreading Marks	
⬭	misspelling
⚌	make a capital letter
⊙	add a period

I am going to the zoo with Bill He sed there are green alligators there. I wont to see the black and yelow giraffes We will have lots of fun.

_____   _____   _____

1. _____ 2. _____ 3. _____

Now find two sentences that should end with a period. Use the correct proofreading mark to show where the periods should be.

 MEANING STRATEGY Write about a snake you have seen in the zoo or the woods. List and use at least four spelling words. Then check your work.

_____   _____

1. _____ 3. _____

_____   _____

2. _____ 4. _____

Often-Misspelled Words

Some words are hard to spell. They may not follow spelling rules. This list shows some of these words. Study them. Learn how to spell them.

A	I	T
are	I	the
		they
C	L	
come	love	W
		want
D	M	was
do	my	where
F	O	Y
for	of	you
from		
H	S	
have	said	
her	some	
here		

Structural Spelling Patterns

Plurals

- Add **–s** to most nouns to make them plural. (cat + s = cats)
- Add **–es** to words that end in *ch, sh, s, ss, x, z,* or *zz.*
- Noticing the syllables in the singular and plural forms of a word can help you know whether to add **–s** or **–es.** When **–es** is added, it usually adds another syllable.

Irregular Plurals

- For words that end in *f* or *fe*, change the *f* to a *v* and add **–es.**
- Some plurals are spelled the same as the singular form, such as *deer.*
- The spelling changes in the plural form of some words, like *tooth* and *teeth.*
- For a word that ends in **consonant-o,** add **–es.** If a word ends in **vowel-o, –s** is usually added.

Continuous Stroke
Handwriting Models

Use these models to help make your writing neat and clear.

Aa Bb Cc Dd Ee

Ff Gg Hh Ii Jj

Kk Ll Mm Nn

Oo Pp Qq Rr Ss

Tt Uu Vv Ww Xx

Yy Zz

Ball and Stick
Handwriting Models

Use these models to help make your writing neat and clear.

Aa Bb Cc Dd Ee

Ff Gg Hh Ii Jj

Kk Ll Mm Nn

Oo Pp Qq Rr Ss

Tt Uu Vv Ww Xx

Yy Zz

Spelling Strategies

There are many different ways to learn how to spell. A spelling strategy is a plan or clue that can make learning to spell easier. These strategies appear in different lessons throughout this book. Take some time to learn how each one can help you to spell better.

SOUND PATTERN STRATEGIES

Pronunciation Strategy
Learn to listen to the sounds in a word. Then spell each sound.

sit

Consonant-Substitution Strategy
Try switching the consonant letters without changing the vowel.

bat, hat, rat, flat, splat/mat, mad, map, mask

Vowel-Substitution Strategy
Try switching the vowel letters without changing the rest of the word.

hit, hat, hut, hot/mane, mine/boat, beat

Rhyming Strategy
Think of a word that rhymes with the spelling word and has the same spelling pattern.

cub, tub, rub

STRUCTURAL PATTERN STRATEGIES

Conventions Strategy
Think about the rules and exceptions you have learned for adding endings to words.

crying, cried

Proofreading Strategy

Check your writing carefully for spelling mistakes you didn't mean to make.

Visualization Strategy

Think about how the word looks. Most words look wrong when they do not have the right spelling.

can not *cen*

MEANING PATTERN STRATEGIES

Family Strategy

Think of how words from the same family are spelled.

art, artist

Meaning Strategy

Think about the meaning of the word to make sure you're using the right word.

see, sea

Compound Word Strategy

Break the compound into its two words to spell each word.

homework, home work

Foreign Language Strategy

Think of foreign language word spellings that are different from English spelling patterns.

ballet

Dictionary Strategy

Find the word in a dictionary to make sure your spelling is correct.

How to Use a Dictionary

A dictionary tells you how to spell a word and what it means. A word can have one or more meanings.

The word you look up in a dictionary is called the *entry word*. Entry words are in alphabetical order.

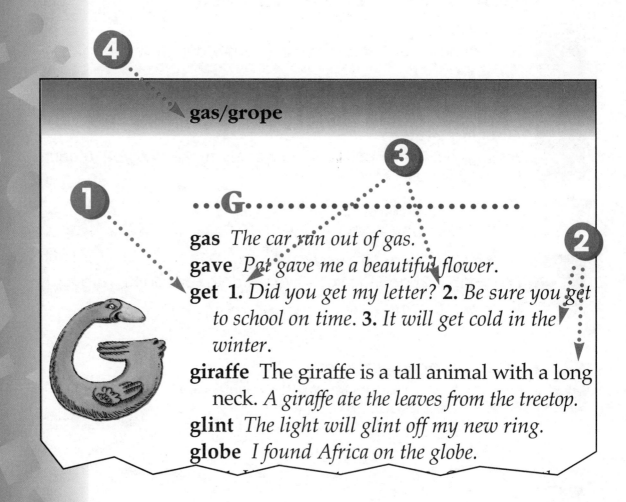

4

gas/grope

3

1

...**G**.......................................

2

gas *The car ran out of gas.*
gave *Pat gave me a beautiful flower.*
get **1.** *Did you get my letter?* **2.** *Be sure you get to school on time.* **3.** *It will get cold in the winter.*
giraffe *The giraffe is a tall animal with a long neck. A giraffe ate the leaves from the treetop.*
glint *The light will glint off my new ring.*
globe *I found Africa on the globe.*

1 The *entry word* is the word you look up. Entry words are in bold type and alphabetical order.

2 Sometimes the entry word is used in a *sample sentence* to help explain its meaning. Sometimes a *definition* is given.

3 When more than one *meaning* is given to an entry word, the meanings are numbered.

4 The two words at the top of each dictionary page are *guide words*. They are the first and last entry words on that page. Guide words help you find an entry word quickly.

Speller Dictionary

···A···················

all 1. *All of the children were on the bus.* **2.** large effort; everything someone has. *She gave the project her all.*

am *I am happy that you came to my house. I am going to read a story.*

and *The apple was big and red. One and one make two.*

are *We are glad we came here. You are playing in my room.* We say: I am, you are, he is, she is, it is, we are, you are, they are.

···B···················

bag A bag is used to hold things. *My father put my lunch in a brown bag.*

bake *Will you bake a cake for my birthday?*

basket A basket is used to hold things. *I put the apples in a basket.*

beaver A beaver is an animal with a large, flat tail and strong teeth. *The beaver cut the tree down with its teeth.*

bee *A bee can fly from flower to flower.*

beg *I had to beg him to give me the book.*

big *Tigers are very big cats. I live in a big city.*

bike *I ride my bike to school each day.*

black *The sky is black at night. The pen on the desk is black.*

blue *Blue is the color of the sky when it is day. Brad and Maria both have blue eyes.*

bone *Drink milk if you want strong bones. The dog played with the bone.*

box A box is used to hold things. *This box is made of wood. The children keep their toys in a wooden box.*

brown *My sister has brown hair. We saw a brown bear in the zoo last week.*

bucket A bucket is used to hold or carry something. *The children filled their buckets with water to help wash the car.*

bug *An ant is one kind of bug. She found a bug in the grass.*

bus *They ride a bus to school.*

but *My dog is big, but your dog is small. You may go to the birthday party, but don't stay out after dark.*

···C·····················

cage A cage is something to keep animals in. *My bird lives in a cage.*

came *All of my friends came to my birthday party.*

can **1.** *You can swim fast.* **2.** *Mom said we can go to the park.* **3.** *Can you fix the TV?* **4.** *She opened the can of paint. The fish we ate for dinner came in a can.*

cat A cat is a small animal that people keep as a pet. *Our cat likes to drink milk.*

chain **1.** *A chain holds my bike to the tree.* **2.** *I chain my dog to a tree so it won't run away.*

chart **1.** *Show how much you grow each year on a chart.* **2.** *Chart the changes in the weather for one week.*

chase To chase means to go or run after. *Dogs like to chase cats.*

chat **1.** *I like to chat with my friends after school.* **2.** *I had a long chat with my sister last night.*

check **1.** *Put a check mark by the red star.* **2.** *Take care when you check your work.*

chest **1.** Your chest is the front part of your body just below the shoulders. *My chest rises when I breathe.* **2.** A chest is also a big box that holds things. *My winter blanket is in the chest.*

chime A chime is a ringing sound. *The clock will chime every hour.*

chin Your chin is part of your face. *My father has a cut on his chin.*

chop **1.** To chop means to cut. *Please chop some wood for the fire.* **2.** A chop is a small cut of meat. *She had a lamb chop for dinner.*

city A city is a place where a lot of people live and work. *We went to the city to see a play.*

clam A clam is a kind of animal that lives in water. *We were looking for a clam in the sand by the sea.*

clan A clan is a group of families. *The people in this clan all have the same great-grandfather.*

clap **1.** *We will clap our hands when the show ends.* **2.** *We heard a clap of thunder.*

class **1.** *There are many children in my class at school.* **2.** *We had fun in science class today.*

clay *There is clay under the sea. He made a cup out of clay.*

clear *Glass is clear. The air is clear.*

clip **1.** *We clip my dog's coat when his hair grows too long.* **2.** *You can hold these papers together with a clip.* **3.** *Please clip these papers together.*

club *My club gets together every day after school.*

clue A clue can help us find an answer to a problem or a mystery. *The footprints were the clue that helped us find the robber.*

code A code is used to send messages. *My friend made up a secret code.*

coffin A coffin is a box in which people are buried. *They lowered the coffin into the grave.*

come *My dog will come to me when I call his name. All of your friends will come to the park.*

crate A crate is a kind of wooden box. *We got a crate of oranges as a gift.*

cub A cub is a very young bear, wolf, lion, or tiger. *We saw lion cubs at the zoo. The polar bear cubs are so cute!*

cup A cup is something to drink from. *I like to drink milk from a cup.*

 **D**

dad *My dad rides a bus to work every day. My dad and I play ball at the park.*

day **1.** *The sky is light when it is day.* **2.** *We had a nice day.*

deep *We dug a deep hole in the sand. The ocean is deep and wide.*

did *Did you see that beautiful bird? Yes, I did.*

dig *Our dog likes to dig for bones in the ground.*

dime *I got a dime for helping my mom. The man in the store will take my dime.*

do **1.** *Please do this work for me.* **2.** *Do you like milk?* **3.** *She swims better than I do.*

dream *I woke up from a sweet dream. Last night I had a dream about my mom.*

··EF···························

earth **1.** *The farmer dug up the earth to plant the crops.* **2. Earth.** *We live on Earth.*

egg **1.** *The baby chicken came out of a chicken egg.* **2.** *I ate an egg salad sandwich.*

elephant An elephant is a large gray animal with a long nose called a trunk. *A baby elephant was the star of the circus.*

fan **1.** *We use a fan in our house when it is hot.* **2.** *My aunt has a pretty paper fan.*

farm A farm is a place where people raise animals and plants. *My uncle lives on a farm and raises sheep.*

feel **1.** *You can feel the water by putting your hand in it.* **2.** *Kim and Reggie feel very happy today.*

feet **1.** *We have two feet for walking.* **2.** *The girl is three feet tall.*

fin A fin is a part of a fish that helps it swim. *Fish move their fins as they swim.*

fine 1. *Everyone liked the fine food.* **2.** *I feel fine today.* **3.** *She got a fine because she did not stop at the red light.*

five *My hand has five fingers. My foot has five toes.*

flag *The flag of our country is red, white, and blue. Juan made a flag for our club.*

flap 1. *The flag began to flap in the wind.* **2.** *The flap on my tent is open.*

flat *We like to ride our bikes on a flat road. Our car has a flat tire.*

fleet *A fleet of ships sailed the sea.*

flip 1. *Let's flip a dime to see who goes first.* **2.** *He did a flip into the pool.*

flood *Everything got wet in the flood. There was a flood in the kitchen when the sink overflowed.*

fly 1. A fly is a kind of bug. *The bird ate a little black fly.* **2.** *We saw the bird fly from one tree to another. I like to fly my kite in the wind.*

for 1. *She went for a walk in the park.* **2.** *He worked here for two days.* **3.** *That box is for toys.* **4.** *He will thank you for the book.*

fox A fox is a wild animal that looks something like a dog. *The fox ran after the rabbit.*

fret To fret means to worry. *Do not fret over spilled milk.*

from 1. *We took a train from one city to the next.* **2.** *Please take that book away from him.* **3.** *His hands are blue from the cold.*

fun *I had fun at your party. That game was a lot of fun.*

···G·························

gas *The car ran out of gas.*

gave *Pat gave me a beautiful flower.*

get 1. *Did you get my letter?* **2.** *Be sure you get to school on time.* **3.** *It will get cold in the winter.*

giraffe The giraffe is a tall animal with a long neck. *A giraffe ate the leaves from the treetop.*

glint *The light will glint off my new ring.*

globe *I found Africa on the globe.*

go 1. *We can go to the zoo.* **2.** *Cars go on the street.* **3.** *Please do not go until the show is over.*

gold 1. Gold is a color. *In the fall, the leaves turn red and gold.* **2.** Gold is a metal. *Dad found gold in the stream.*

gorilla A gorilla is a large, strong animal. *The gorilla ate an apple. A gorilla is a shy animal.*

got 1. *I got a new coat today.* **2.** *I got tired waiting for you.*

gray Gray is a color that is made by mixing black and white. *Grandma has gray hair.*

green 1. *The leaves on that plant are green. Bess has green eyes.* **2.** Green means not ripe. *I do not like green bananas.*

grid A grid is made of lines. *Put the numbers in a grid.*

grip To grip means to hold tight. *I will grip the bat and swing at the ball.*

grope To grope means to feel your way in the dark. *I had to grope my way in the dark room.*

gruff To be gruff means to be mean. *Please be nice, not gruff.*

••**H**••••••••••••••••••••

had **1.** *She had a birthday party last night.* **2.** *I had a cold, but now I feel better.*

hamper *Put your dirty socks in the clothes hamper.*

has *Betty has a new book. A tiger has sharp teeth.*

have **1.** *I have a big dog.* **2.** *We have to leave for school now.* **3.** *Please have this room cleaned.* **4.** *Will you have milk or water?*

hay *Cows and horses eat hay.*

he *Mr. Green is old, but he can still swim faster than I can.*

hen *We leave seeds for the hen to eat.*

her **1.** *I gave her my book.* **2.** *Have you seen her today?* **3.** *Her dog is in the house.*

here **1.** *I will wait for my mother and my sister right here.* **2.** *The children come here to have fun.* **3.** *Where should I go from here?*

hero A hero is a good, brave person. *Shirley Chisholm was my hero when I was a little girl.*

hide To hide means to keep from being seen. *I'll hide the birthday cake so it will be a surprise. When we play, she will hide first.*

hill A hill is a high area of land. *We can walk our bikes up the hill.*

him **1.** *I let him ride my bike.* **2.** *Jim wants to go, so take him with you.* **3.** *Give him some milk.*

home A home is a place to live. *I go home every day after school. My home is at 6 Pine Road.*

hop *Can you hop on your right foot? Rabbits hop from one place to another as they look for food.*

hope *I hope you feel better very soon. I hope the rain stops so we can go to the zoo.*

hot *The sun is very hot. That fire was hot. We were hot from playing outside.*

huff To be in a huff means to be angry. *If you hurt me again, I will get in a huff.*

hug **1.** *The little girl wanted to hug my kitten.* **2.** *The boy gave his dad a hug.*

••IJ••••••••••••••••••••

I *I am six today. I feel fine. I like my new friend.*

in **1.** *The dog is in the house. Put the toy in the box.* **2.** *It snows in the winter.*

is **1.** *She is six.* **2.** *Father is not home now. Is that you at the door?*

it **1.** *My friend threw the ball and I caught it.* **2.** *It is raining outside.*

jeep A jeep is a small car. *Tom rides in a jeep because the roads are snowy.*

jet **1.** *A jet of water came out of the tap.* **2.** *You can fly to another country in a jet.*

job *It is my job to take out the trash. My sister's job is to set the table.*

joke A joke is something that makes people laugh. **1.** *Jeff told a funny joke and everyone laughed.* **2.** *At school we joke with our friends.*

...KL...........................

keg *There is something to drink in the keg.*

kite *My kite is flying in the wind.*

lake A lake is water with land all around it.
We swim in the lake during the summer.

lantern A lantern is a light to carry with you.
Bring a lantern on a night walk.

law A law is a rule made by the government
of a city, state, or country. *Our town has a
law against littering.*

lay **1.** *Please lay that book on the table.* **2.** *Our
hen will lay an egg soon.* **3.** *We lay on the grass
watching the clouds.*

learn *In school we learn to read and write. Each
student will learn at her own pace.*

leg **1.** *Can you stand on one leg?* **2.** *The leg of the
chair is white.*

like **1.** *Dogs like bones. I like you very much.*
2. *Tad is dressed like a clown.*

lime A lime is a small, sour, green fruit. *Don
likes lime in his soda.*

line **1.** *I drew a line with a red crayon.* **2.** *I have
to stand in line for the bus.*

lock **1.** *Please lock the door after you close it.*
2. *Bring the key for the lock.*

...M...........................

magnet A magnet is a piece of metal that
sticks to other metals. *Frank used his magnet
to pick up the nails that spilled.*

mass 1. *A mass of people came to see our show.* **2.** *A mountain has a lot of mass.*

may 1. *May I leave now? May I have some paper?* **2.** *The man said that it may snow today.*

me *Please give me an apple. My sister takes me to school every day.*

mean *Please do not be mean to your sister.*

mine 1. *The hat on the table is mine. The red bike is yours; mine is blue.* **2.** *My father works in a gold mine.* **3.** *I also mine for gold.*

mole A mole is a small, soft animal. *A mole dug a hole in the lawn.*

mom *My mom is a doctor. Ask your mom if you can go to the zoo next week.*

mug *My mug has cocoa in it.*

my *My house is near the park. Ted is my brother. That is my book on the table.*

···N····················

name 1. *My mother's name is Kate.* **2.** *I will name my cat Tiger.*

need *I need new shoes this year. My sister needs a new fancy dress.*

net *Many fish were in my net. Kim hit the ball over the net.*

news News is the story of something that just happened. *Did you read the news about the fire at the factory?*

nine *Eight and one is nine. Ten minus one is nine.*

no 1. *Can you come? No, I can't.* **2.** *There is no school today.*

not *My brother is not home now. It did not rain last night. One and one are two, not three.*

note 1. *The note told me where to find my mother. Please make a note of this.* **2.** *Please note what I am doing now.*

number *My favorite number is 7.*

nut *The squirrel is eating a nut.*

···OP·····················

orange 1. *I ate an orange after lunch.* **2.** Orange is a color that is a mix of yellow and red. *In the fall, some leaves turn orange.*

otter An otter is a water animal. *That otter is playing in the water.*

pet 1. *This dog is my pet.* **2.** *We will pet the kitten all day.*

pig A pig is an animal that you may find in the country. *My little brother has a toy pig.*

pink Pink is a color that is a mix of red and white. *The flowers I picked are pink.*

play 1. *May we play at your house today?* **2.** *I like to play the piano.* **3.** *I saw a funny play.*

plot A plot is the main story in a book or movie. *In the plot of this story, the princess asks the prince to marry her.*

pole *The flag was on top of a tall pole.*

pop 1. *We heard a pop when our car got a flat tire.* **2.** *The tire popped with a big noise.* **3.** *The clown will pop out of the box.*

pot *My mother cooks food in a big pot. I have a pot of flowers in my room.*

purple Purple is a color that is a mix of red and blue. *She has purple shoes.*

...R.........................

ran *Mike ran all the way to school.*

red *Stop at the red light. I saw a red fire truck.*

ride **1.** *I ride my bike to the park.* **2.** *We will take a ride into the country.*

rode *He rode his bike over to my house.*

rope **1.** *I like to jump with this rope.* **2.** *Can you rope these boxes together?*

run **1.** *My father had to run to catch the bus. That dog likes to run after my ball.* **2.** *When our car was broken, it wouldn't run.*

rust **1.** *There is rust on my bike.* **2.** *The car may rust if it is left out in the rain.*

...S.........................

said *Jan said "Hello" to her friend. She said that she would be here soon.*

sand *I played in the sand at the beach.*

sat *Mom sat in your chair. I sat in the car.*

see **1.** *When you close your eyes you cannot see. See that star in the sky?* **2.** *I do not see why you must go now.* **3.** *Please see who is at the door.* **4.** *Let's see a show.*

seed *If you plant this seed, a flower will grow.*

shape **1.** *A box is not the same shape as a ball.* **2.** *She was in bad shape after she fell.* **3.** *I can shape the clay into a ball.*

share To share means to give some of what you have to someone else. *Roberto said he would share his cookies with us.*

shark A shark is a big fish that eats other fish. *The boat was not near the shark.*

she *My mother says she likes to run. Bess told me she would come to my party.*

shell *My pet turtle has a green shell. The shell of this nut is hard to crack.*

shelter *We ate our picnic in the shelter because it was raining.*

sheriff *In the movie, the sheriff put the bad guys in jail. The sheriff has a badge shaped like a star.*

shine To shine means to give out light. *The sun shines all the time.*

ship **1.** A ship is a big boat. *I saw the sea from the ship.* **2.** *I will ship this box to my friend.*

shop **1.** A shop is a store. *I saw a kitten in the pet shop.* **2.** *I will shop for a new coat today.*

silt Silt is fine sand or clay that is carried in water. *The silt in the river made it look brown. The silt fell to the bottom of the river.*

silver Silver is a shiny metal. *My mother gave me a silver ring. We eat from silver spoons.*

sit *May I sit on that chair? My leg hurts so I must sit down. My cat likes to sit in the sun.*

size **1.** *The two balls are the same size.* **2.** *My shoe size is six.*

skip *I learned to skip when I was four. I can skip faster than I can walk.*

skit A skit is a short play. *Our parents loved the class skit.*

snail A snail is a small animal that moves very slowly. *Most snails have brown shells.*

snake *The snake moved slowly along the ground.*

snap **1.** *Did you hear the wood on the fire snap?* **2.** *The rope may snap if the dog pulls hard.* **3.** *The dog may snap at you.* **4.** *The box of toys closed with a snap.* **5.** *She snapped her fingers.*

sneeze *When I have a cold I sneeze a lot.*

sniff To sniff is to smell. *I will sniff the pie when it comes out of the oven.*

snore *I snore in my sleep when I have a cold. My dad snored all night long.*

snow **1.** *Snow fell all day today.* **2.** *I think it will snow again tomorrow.*

snug **1.** *It is nice to get into a snug bed on a cold night.* **2.** *These shoes are a little too snug.*

some **1.** *Some birds cannot sing. I can see some of the boys. Please have some milk before you go.* **2.** *I will keep some and give you the others.*

speed **1.** *The race car can speed out of sight.* **2.** *The airplane flew at a great speed.*

star *I saw a star in the night sky.*

stay **1.** *Please stay here. The dog will stay in the house all day.* **2.** *We came home after a stay with my grandma.*

stem A stem is part of a plant. *The rose has a long stem.*

step **1.** *I can do that dance step. I was a step from the door when my mother called me.* **2.** *The store is only a step away from your house.* **3.** *I fell down the steps.* **4.** *The man told everyone to step to the back. Don't step on that ant!*

stick A stick is a long, thin piece of wood. *I threw a stick, and my dog ran after it.*

sting *The bee sting on my foot hurts.*

stock **1.** *Stock the shelves with apples and pears.* **2.** *The store has a large stock of toys.*

stone *That house is made of stone. Ben painted a stone red.*

stop **1.** *A car must stop at a red light. We will stop at the park.* **2.** *The rain may stop soon. She asked us to stop making noise.* **3.** *The bus made a stop at our school. The bus stop is near my new house.*

stove *My dad cooks food on the stove. This stove burns wood.*

subtraction *Taking 3 from 7 to get 4 is called subtraction.*

sum *The sum of 3 and 4 is 7.*

sun **1.** *The sun gives us light.* **2.** *My kitten likes to sleep in the sun.*

···**T**························

take **1.** *Ann will take the book off the table.* **2.** *My mom and dad take a bus to work.* **3.** *Please take us to the movies!*

tan *My skin will tan in the sun.*

that **1.** *Did you see that?* **2.** *That girl is my friend.*

the *Please close the window. The boy in the car is my brother.*

then **1.** *The show ended, and then we clapped.* **2.** *I hope you will do the work by then.* **3.** *If she*

did all of the work, then she should get all of the money.

these 1. *I like these shoes.* **2.** *These are my socks.*

they *Mark and Matt did not come because they missed the bus. Do you know where they are?*

thin *A hair is thin. I only want a thin slice of cheese.*

this *I like this cat. This book is mine, and that book is yours.*

those 1. *The children played with those toys.* **2.** *Those are her books and these are my books.*

three 1. *Two and one are three.* **2.** *Four minus one is three.*

throw 1. *Throw the ball to the dog, and she will bring it back to you.* **2.** *If the milk smells bad, you should throw it away.*

time 1. *A long time ago people cooked on wood stoves.* **2.** *What time is it?* **3.** *We had a good time at your party.*

top 1. *We ran to the top of the hill.* **2.** A top is a kind of toy. *He watched the top go around.*

town A town is a place where people live and work. *Our town has a park on the main street.*

tree A tree is a plant that has a trunk. *I will climb the tree and sit in the branches.*

tub *Mom filled the tub with water. Sit in that tub until you are clean.*

···UVW················

us *Uncle Ben took us to the zoo yesterday. Our teacher let us go outside.*

vase *Put the flower in the vase with some water.*

vine A vine is a plant with a thin, very long stem. *A vine grows along the brick wall.*

violet Violet is a color. *I used a violet crayon to color the flowers.*

vote *I will vote for Gina for class president.*

want *Kim and I want to get a kitten. Do you want more milk?*

was **1.** *I was at her party last night.* **2.** *Everyone was singing the song.* **3.** *The food was good.*

waves *Her dive made waves in the pool.*

way *She showed us the way to make cookies.*

we *We both like ice cream.*

web *There was a fly in the web.*

weed **1.** *Please pull that weed out of the ground.* **2.** *Tim will weed the garden.*

were **1.** *We were having fun in the park and we did not want to come home.* **2.** *We were going to see that movie, but we didn't.*

wet **1.** *My coat was wet from the rain.* **2.** *Do not put your hand on the wet paint.*

whale A whale is a big animal that has the shape of a fish. *We saw a whale in the sea.*

wheel *There are four wheels on my wagon. A bike has two wheels.*

when **1.** *When do you start school?* **2.** *I will come when you call me.* **3.** *We have only three pictures when we need six.*

where **1.** *Where did you put the book? Where does she live?* **2.** *Your coat is where you put it.*

which **1.** *Which book did you like best?* **2.** *The coat, which I showed you, is very old.*

whisper To whisper means to speak in a quiet voice. *I will whisper a secret in your ear.*

white *The paper is white. The clean, white snow fell on the ground.*

why **1.** *Why did he laugh? I don't know why Jill can't come with us.* **2.** *Why, look who just got here!*

wide *The chair is too wide to fit through the door.*

win **1.** *I hope you win the money. The fastest one will win the race.* **2.** *The school soccer team has one win and one loss.*

XYZ

yellow *The sun is yellow. The old paper has turned yellow.*

yes *Yes, you are right. Yes, you may go to the zoo.*

you *Do you want to come with me? You push down the top to open the box.*